Shaping the Culture of Schooling

SUNY Series, Education and Culture: Critical Factors in the Formation of Character and Community in American Life

Eugene F. Provenzo, Jr. and Paul Farber, editors

Shaping the Culture of Schooling

The Rise of
Outcome-Based
Education

CHERYL TAYLOR DESMOND

STATE UNIVERSITY
OF NEW YORK PRESS

The following have generously given permission to reprint excerpts from copyrighted works.

Excerpt from "Choruses from the Rock" in *Collected Poems 1909–1962* by T. S. Eliot, copyright 1936 by Harcourt Brace & Company, copyright © 1963 by T. S. Eliot, reprinted by permission of the publisher.

Excerpt from "Mastery Learning, Boon to Upstate City, Stirs Wide Interest," by Robert W. Vogle, copyright © 1980 by the New York Times Company, reprinted by permission.

Excerpt from "Johnson City's Philosophical Principles and Practices," *Outcomes* 2 (1), with permission from John R. Champlin and Albert Mamary.

Fig. 1, (p. 4), fig. 2, (p. 88), fig. 3, (p. 89), and fig. 4, (p. 109) disseminated at the Conference on Outcome-Based Education/ODDM, reprinted with permission.

Published by
State University of New York Press

© 1996 State University of New York

For information, address the State University of New York Press, State University Plaza, Albany, NY 12246

Production by Bernadine Dawes • Marketing by Fran Keneston

Library of Congress Cataloging-in-Publication Data

Desmond, Cheryl Taylor, 1948—
    Shaping the culture of schooling : the rise of outcome-based ecucation / Cheryl Taylor Desmond.
        p.   cm. — (SUNY series, education and culture)
    Includes bibliographical references and index.
    ISBN 0-7914-2955-5 (HC : alk. paper). — ISBN 0-7914-2956-3 (PB : alk. paper)
    1. Competency based education—New York (State)—Johnson City—History.
    2. Community and school—New York (State)—Johnson City—History.
    3. School management and organization—New York (State)—Johnson City—History. I. Title. II. Series.

LC1032.5.N69D47   1996
370'.9747'75—dc20   95-44256
                                                                         CIP

Contents

Foreword

The tradition of looking at innovative school systems and their potential to act as models for educational reform dates back to the nineteenth century. In the early 1940s, as part of the Common School Movement, reformers such a Calvin Stowe, Alexander Bache, and Horace Mann turned to European schools for new ideas. In the 1890s, Joseph Mayer Rice looked to innovative school systems such as Quincy, Massachusetts for educational models that could be used throughout the country.

This tradition has continued into the twentieth century. In 1915, John Dewey and his daughter Evelyn Dewey published *Schools of Tomorrow*—perhaps the most famous study of innovative schools and their potential to provide models for school reform and improvement. In the 1960s, A. S. Neil's *Summerhill: A Radical Approach to Childrearing* provided educators with a detailed account of a highly innovative educational model at work.

In general, the literature on innovative schools is descriptive and lacks detailed analysis. It does little to contextualize the schools it describes and assumes that the innovations it describes are useful and valid. Cheryl Desmond's *Shaping the Culture of Schooling* is, in many respects, a continuation of this tradition of describing innovative schools at work. But it is also an important departure from this tradition as it tries to link the innovations that are being observed and described to a larger cultural and theoretical context. Desmond examines the rise of outcome-based education in the context of the people who were most responsible for developing these programs in the Johnson City (New York) public schools, as well as in the context of the local community's development and its historical links to companies such as Endicott Johnson and the IBM Corporation.

Desmond's work, while largely historical, is also an ethnographic and policy study. It draws heavily on interpretive models from critical theorists such as Apple and Giroux and from economists such as Carnoy and Levin. Unlike earlier works on educational innovation, it asks questions about who benefits "in" and "from" schooling, about teacher empowerment, about the role of community and industry in defining the meaning of schooling, about how the struggle for power reshapes the praxis of school leadership, and about what defines the public good in a democratic society.

This is an important and insightful book. It warrants careful attention in the research literature not only because it is the interesting story of a promising educational innovation, but also because it is a detailed examination of how educational reform actually works in the context of a specific community over an extended period of time. This is a book that practitioners in the field will find useful and that researchers will find essential in attempting to better understand how education reforms are implemented and disseminated across broader settings.

Eugene F. Provenzo

Preface

"All wind and little rain" may be an apt phrase to characterize the extensive efforts to reform American schools in the past several decades. Each year new educational programs are heralded in American schools just as the past year's innovation whimpers into dormancy. One of the few exceptions to this general rule in American schooling is in Johnson City, New York, where the schools have sustained positive, meaningful educational change for children since 1964. The Johnson City schools have also given birth to the national movement of outcome-based education. Why has the reform of the Johnson City schools been the exception to the dismal failures of school reform in other communities?

To find out, this book examines the historical and cultural development of school change in Johnson City to determine what happened in Johnson City, why and how this happened, and what can be learned about instructional change from the Johnson City experience. To understand the reform of the Johnson City schools required a look back to the town's creation as a model community in the 1890s; it reveals that school change is slow and not gentle; it is complex and paradoxical, and therefore unpredictable. School change demands an intense, inclusive commitment within the school-community as well as in the economic, political, and social community surrounding the school. Conflicting, paradoxical forces continually rub the fabric of school and community and create tense dilemmas for the decision makers within any school and community, but especially for those trying to change traditions and practices. By giving both face and voice to those initiating, resisting, and accepting change, the book analyzes the culture and conditions of school and community that cause, block, or permit change. It also reveals that the heart of positive school reform lies in the person-to-person mediation of the knowledge that children have virtually unlimited learning capacity; it lies in a synergistic relationship of power and commitment by leaders, teachers, learners, and citizens.

In the book, I interweave the rise of outcome-based education with the personal, daily work of the people who have shaped the culture of both community and school. Like all schools, the Johnson City schools are tightly interconnected with the overt and covert values of the surrounding community. Johnson City began as a cooperative industrial commonwealth that celebrated the working-class values of hard work and mutual concern but had little regard for formal education. The work of those who labored in the schools changed this disregard and reshaped the culture into one that valued educational attainment.

In my efforts to describe and analyze the constantly swirling, messy interrelated contexts of the school and community in which these changes have occurred, I have been influenced by the theoretical work of Apple, of Giroux, and of Carnoy and Levin. Apple and Giroux have both maintained that the family, the workplace, the social and political community, and the school are active cultural sites that both sustain and resist the dominant economic, political, and social ideologies and are interrelated in paradoxical ways.[1] Carnoy and Levin have extended this interpretation of the ongoing tension in American life as part of the "wider social conflict . . . in the nature of capitalist production . . . in a politically democratic society," but have reemphasized the role of economic resources in the injustices of schooling.[2]

In examining the continuing evolving relationship of community and schools, I attempt to extend the scrutiny of "individualism and commitment in American life and the search for meaning in private and public life" explored so deftly by Bellah et al. in *Habits of the Heart*, their study of late-twentieth-century Americans.[3] The conflict experienced in Johnson City as one economic ethos supplanted another and initiated educational reform calls into question what is gained and what is lost as industrial communities make way for global networks, and hints at what may be necessary culturally if we want to "return in a new way to the idea of work in schools and communities as a contribution to the good of all and not merely as a means to one's advancement."[4]

The re-forming of school and community also illuminates the continuous process of the negotiation and renegotiation of the meaning of self and others in the contexts of the workplace, community, and school within a political democracy, and captures the reciprocating, dialectical actions of power in response to complex problems during conflict and during stasis. The quiet movement of the constant processing of meaning for humans who work in schools and in communities is an essential element that must be considered when viewing and analyzing the transformation of Johnson City from an industrial community to a technologically based economy, from a school for future factory workers to an outcome-based education for all students.

This book is the culmination of research begun in 1985.[5] Originally, the study began as an investigation of the political dynamics of the school board and superintendent relationship in the development of Johnson City's model of outcome-based education. However, the nature of the study deepened with a discovery made in March 1986. During one of my early visits to the district, another visitor, a superintendent from California and a native son of Johnson City, explained to me the origin of the unusual names of the elementary school ("Harry L.") and the middle school ("George F."). He recounted how the schools had been named after members of the Johnson family. He also described how the Johnsons had founded the town and owned the Endicott Johnson Shoe Corporation. Fascinated by his tales of Endicott Johnson, I subsequently began to research the history of the community and the paternalism of the Endicott Johnson Corporation. The strong influence of this corporation upon the school district could not be ignored. Thus, a study begun as a political analysis of school leadership and reform developed into a cultural history of the relationship of community and school in school reform.

For this reason, the methodology of the study has followed the guidelines of historical method but has also included qualitative and political analysis. While researching the school district and community of Johnson City from 1986 through 1989, I interfaced my own data with an array of studies conducted by faculty and students at Syracuse University and by school district employees upon student achievement, attitudes, and attendance; district programs; district staff; and the history of the Endicott Johnson Corporation and International Business Machines. My appreciation goes to Tom Rusk Vickery and John Briggs of Syracuse University and to the school employees and community of Johnson City for granting me unlimited access to these studies, publications, and files of data.

My historical investigation of Johnson City and its interpretation has been guided by Lukacs's concept of history as "the remembered—and not merely the recorded—past."[6] In his work on historical consciousness, Lukacs stated that the "very purpose of historical knowledge is . . . a certain kind of understanding: historical knowledge is the knowledge of human beings about other human beings." History encompasses all kinds of records of the past and the "remembered past is a much larger category than the recorded past."[7] Lukacs explained that the remembered past is not history as memory, but that its meaning

> involves that complexities of what *remembering* is together with the complexities of what is the *past*. The functions of human remembering—what and how and why some things are remembered—are fantastically complex, because our memory is personal and because we are historical beings. But the past, too, is something that cannot be stowed away into a simple, definite, closed category. It is not as completely irrevocable as it may seem.[8]

According to Lukacs, our improvement of our understanding of the past comes not only with our own accumulation of experiences but with our learning of "different and newly revealed things about a particular incident from others—other participants, observers, reporters, historians. For historical thinking is the constant, the frequent *rethinking* of the past.[9]

This conception of historical consciousness and of humans' frequent rethinking of the past has been particularly useful in my understanding of the evolution of outcome-based education in Johnson City. It provided insight into the varying and changing conceptions of the history of the school, the community, and the reforms over a thirty-year period. Some of these conceptions had been crafted into an organizational saga by the time I began my research of the district in 1986, just after the district's program was validated by the U.S. Department of Education.

As defined by Clark, an organizational saga

> is a collective understanding of unique accomplishment in a formally established group. . . . [It] presents some rational explanation of how certain means led to certain ends, but it also includes affect that turns a formal place into beloved institution, to which participants may be passionately devoted.[10]

By 1986, fifteen years after the initiation of educational reform, the story of Johnson City's educational successes had been crafted through the district's reports of its achievement in various publications, in its annual conference, and in the efforts to disseminate its reform to other school districts. In my research I wanted to investigate and record the events of and different perspectives on the development of this saga; I wanted to hear the story through various human voices—those recorded in documents and those still in the process of historical rethinking.

The recorded past of the Johnson City Central School District and Johnson City included both published and unpublished school and community documents.

School district documents comprised (1) school-board minutes from 1960 to 1988, with random review of minutes from 1924 through 1959, (2) superintendents' support folders prepared for board members, (3) district external reports, (4) district internal reports, (5) reports of citizen advisory councils appointed by the superintendents, (6) school communications with the community, including newsletters and letters, (7) miscellaneous research reports and letters, (8) school budgets, (9) school-board election results, and (10) annual financial referenda.

Community documents included (1) articles from the Binghamton-based *Sun-Bulletin* and *Evening Press*, now combined as the *Press & Sun-Bulletin*; (2) the history collections of the Binghamton, Endicott, and Johnson City libraries, including local publications, photographs, letters, and local newspaper clippings; (3) the 1967 comprehensive planning document for Johnson City; (4) planning documents for a new comprehensive plan for the community; and (5) U.S. Census data for Johnson City in 1960, 1970, 1977, 1980, and 1990.

I collected statements about the remembered past from Johnson City residents, school-board members, and district employees through formal and informal interviews. In several instances, my interview questions were drawn from data gathered in documents. The documents proved helpful in establishing events that, in preliminary interviews, the interviewees had not mentioned. For example, the labor conflict with the teachers' union in 1976 had not been included in the saga. Only in subsequent interviews when I referenced this period of conflict did school employees recount the full impact of these events upon the progress of the school change. Lukacs's conception of historical consciousness was especially useful in interpreting such untidy aspects with his elucidation of the interrelationship of the recorded and remembered past and the open category of the past.

My data for the study was collected during two-day or three-day visits in the school district in the years 1986 through 1989. During these visits, I reviewed district and community documentation, interviewed faculty, staff, and current school-board members, observed elementary and secondary classes in the district, and attended school-board meetings and a district conference on outcome-based education. In addition, during the summers of 1987 and 1988 I lived with a family in Johnson City for extended periods of a week or more. This family introduced me to the community members and the former school board members, whom I interviewed. As a result of these introductions, I was able to avoid being seen by community members as an emissary of the district from whom they might withhold information or alter it. I also returned to the school district in November 1991 and January 1992 to conduct interviews of staff and faculty for a study on their use of performance assessment of students and integrated curriculum.[11] In November 1993 I also attended the National Conference on Outcome-based Education conducted by former and current district employees.

The coding protocols of the interviews, observations, and documents followed the scheme presented by Bogdan and Biklen in their text on qualitative methods.[12] My analysis of political and economic indicators has been guided by the work of Minar, Lutz and Iannacone, and McGivney.[13] This triangulation of data, of multiple investigators, and of method allowed for the multifaceted nature of school reform, its complexity, and the ever-present possibility of a variable that so often thwarts intended educational change.

As the story of Johnson City and outcome-based education reveals, the historical evolution of change in school and community contains inherently complex, interrelated paradoxes and challenges, ofttimes masked or lost in the glow of a saga of organizational reform and most notably, in the highly rated successes and promises of OBE. If they are not included in the saga of OBE, the reform of the Johnson City schools, like that of reforms of other successful districts, will stand alone, unreplicated, mocking the frantic scurrying of those who profess to change American schools.

The introduction of the book provides an overview of the Johnson City model of outcome-based education and contextualizes this reform in the national educational reform frenzy of the 1980s and 1990s.

Chapter 1 examines the question of "cui bono?"—meaning who benefits in and from schooling. How we answer this question reveals our beliefs about student achievement. It establishes the rationale for the theoretical framework and the social-institutional context necessary to understand the educational change of mastery learning and its successor, outcome-based education, in the Johnson City schools and its implications for school change generally.

Chapter 2 examines the cultural ground of Johnson City as one of the overlapping layers of the social-institutional context of the Johnson City schools. This cultural ground is developed in the economic history and industrial ethos of the Endicott Johnson Corporation. It explores the dilemma of self and community within the economic framework of a community and its work ethos.

Chapter 3 establishes the social contextual factors of demographics and size as they influenced the Johnson City schools and educational change in general. It also explores the ethos of International Business Machines, located in the nearby town of Endicott, and its impact upon the schools. The social dilemma of the self in relationship to all within a community and its sustainability is explored.

Chapter 4 examines the centralization of the Johnson City schools and the development of a new vision for the schools. It explores the meaning of the public good in an American democracy as rational planning replaced paternalism as the integrated principle of the school community.

Chapter 5 probes the questions of who rules within a school district and with what justification as the struggle for power reshapes the praxis of the school leadership.

Chapters 6 and 7 follow the development of the power/knowledge relationship in mastery learning and the shift in Johnson City schools from a paradigm of scarcity to one of synergy.

Chapter 8 examines the inner layers of the social institutional context as school and community interrelate to shape a conception of power as a shared relationship, and examines how this discourse of power was facilitated in the leadership of the Johnson City schools.

Chapter 9 looks at the process of staff development and its role in the development of a synergistic educational paradigm. It demonstrates how the application of mediated learning and an ethic of caring provided the power within for the teachers of Johnson City and the means for the deep systematic adoption of instructional reform.

Chapter 10 places the cultural analysis of the educational reform in Johnson City within the national context of OBE. It argues that the prospect for synergistic reform of schools relies upon our understanding of these three significant aspects of schooling: the daily work of human action and language, ethical relationship, and the deep culture of the school community.

Introduction

The vice principal looked up at the ceiling and then down to his huge, clasped hands as he recollected growing up in Johnson City, New York, during the 1940s. A former semiprofessional football player and the son of an Endicott Johnson (EJ) Shoe factory worker, he thought over each of his words carefully. He was hesitant to be interviewed without the "boss's" permission, so he lingered cautiously in the doorway. He avoided answering my questions about the Johnson City Central School District and its nationally recognized model of outcome-based education (OBE). Among the first school districts in the country to develop and implement outcome-based education, Johnson City was the only one to have implemented successfully the model from kindergarten through twelfth grade.

He chose, instead, to speak of the community and the schooling of his childhood:

> In those days, the IBM kids were the ones who were told to be something—engineers, doctors, lawyers, to go to college. We, EJ kids, were told by our parents and teachers to behave, to stay out of trouble, to finish school. If we did, a job at EJ would be waiting for us.[1]

He spoke of the different lives IBM and EJ families led in the small urban village of seventeen thousand inhabitants. Main Street was the dividing line between the northside homes of the EJ workers of eastern and southern European descent and the southside homes of

1

the IBM employees of English and Irish descent. The Main Street bankers, lawyers, doctors, and merchants treated the "IBMers" and "EJers" differently. He stated that if it had not been for the Korean War and the GI Bill affording him the opportunity to go to college and play semipro ball, he, too, would have been an EJ factory worker, just like his older brother.

These recollections of life in Johnson City appeared at first as diversionary tactics, useful in avoiding my pointed questions on outcome-based education and its beginnings in Johnson City. But remembrances like these of the vice principal and of the many people connected with the school district and community gradually pulled at the neat selvage of the school-based change known as OBE. The unraveling edge revealed the threads of a historical, complex relationship between community and school that shaped the reform of the school district's mission, programs, and curriculum. Each new, unraveled bit of thread pointed to same question: How did this aging industrial, predominately blue-collar community with its "greaser" schools manage to create and sustain successful educational change when most school-reform efforts, often in wealthier, more highly educated communities, collapse in "predictable failure?"[2]

Since 1964, the Johnson City School District had transformed itself from a school preparing mainly EJ factory workers with some IBMers into a model school program for achievement-oriented, technologically able youth. In 1985, its model of outcome-based education, the Outcomes-Driven Developmental Model (ODDM), was validated by the Joint Dissemination Review Panel of the U.S. Office of Education as an exemplary program of sustained school change, K–8, worthy of dissemination throughout the United States.[3] As defined in district documents:

> ODDM is, in essence, a master plan for improving all facets of school operation in order to produce excellent student achievement for all students. The plan calls for a school to "change fully on a small scale" since most school improvement efforts fail due to piecemeal and fragmented efforts.
>
> ODDM is a program for making all schools more effective by ensuring that the conditions exist in which all students can learn with excellence, all teachers can teach more effectively, and all administrators can manage more competently. Through ODDM, JC [Johnson City] sought high levels of achievement for all students in all areas of learning, K–12.[4]

As shown in figure 1, the conceptual model of ODDM is directed by the mission that "all students will learn well" and includes all components of the educational system including students, teachers, administration, and community. Five student exit behaviors are sought as the outcomes of the implementation of the model: (1) self-esteem as learner and person, (2) high cognitive levels, (3) self-directed learner, (4) concern for others, and (5) the process skills of problem solving, communication, decision making, accountability, and group process.

The district's substantial gains in student cognitive achievement were a strong reason for its validation by the U.S. Department of Education. Since 1980, at least 75 percent of Johnson City's eighth-grade students were six months or more above grade level in mathematics; since 1982, the same gains had been accomplished for 75 percent of its eighth-grade students in reading.[5]

The validation of Johnson City's success in significantly improving its schools and the subsequent publicity could not have arrived at a better time for many of the beleaguered leaders in American education.[6] The release of the highly critical reform report on public schools, *A Nation At Risk*, in 1983 and of the innumerable, critical reports, articles, and essays that followed in its wake had blindsided local, state, and national educators.[7] An American public fraught with anxiety that its children were not being prepared to compete in the global marketplace beseiged educators with their concerns. Political and business leaders blamed the decline of the American economy upon the American school. Angry parents screamed for vouchers to send their children to private schools. Financially pressed taxpayers squeezed the schools more than ever. All insisted on "results." The public wanted measurable proof that its children were learning and that the future workers of the country were not "mediocre" dullards, incapable of maintaining America's economic and political greatness.

By the early 1980s the United States had become acutely aware of Japan's emergence as an economic superpower. The country that the United States had first defeated and then rebuilt had arrived on our shores with the number-one selling car; had built a trade surplus of steel, electronics, automobiles, tools, small appliances, and so forth; and had hooked our children on mindless video games. Searching for explanations, American businesses and the public linked our economic sluggishness to American schools and blamed the poor performance of American products on the poor academic preparation of American workers. Severely criticizing American schools for getting

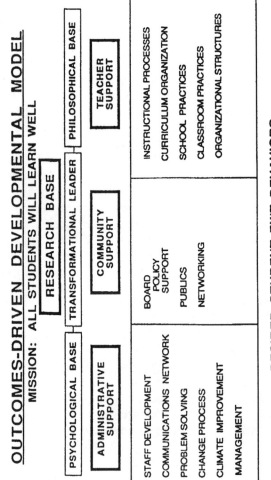

Fig. 1. Reprinted with permission from the Johnson City Schools, 1990.

the country into such a fix, American government and business indicated that Americans were ready to spend more money on their schools, but only if educators could demonstrate that extra funding led to hard data on student achievement gains.

Goals, objectives, and wishes were not enough. Americans had already spent massive amounts of dollars on American schooling during the 1960s and early 1970s to stay ahead of the Soviets and to equalize our schools, but studies like Coleman's had indicated that other factors, not money, were the primary determinants of student achievement.[8] SAT scores had actually declined since 1964; urban schools had only gotten worse; statistically, American children were learning less in school. What the American public wanted and needed were "results," bottom-line indicators that American schools and teachers were capable of increasing children's learning and achieving academic excellence.

Coming out of the politically turbulent period of the civil rights era and the Vietnam War, Americans blamed a decade of schooling that had emphasized educational relevance, process learning, and student self-esteem and self-indulgence for the educational losses that were tallied in national and local reports. Americans leaned more and more toward the conservative agenda of the political and educational Right in Reagan's "morning in America." "Warm fuzzies" were not in the geopolitical, economic interest of the nation. American schools needed to demonstrate that American children had the "right stuff," the brains and skills to beat the Japanese economically and hold off our aging but still-present enemy, the Soviets.

The achievement gains of Johnson City's children were just the positive bottom-line indicators the doctor ordered. Hearing of and reading about these educational outcomes, educators desperate to improve the schools began swarming to Johnson City. They visited district classrooms, sought the advice of its staff, and flocked to its local conferences. All were eager to find solutions for the ailing, humiliated American public schools. By the end of the 1986–87 school year, over eight hundred educators from the United States, Canada, and Europe had visited the district; several hundred more had attended its fall and spring conferences on the Outcomes Driven Developmental Model (ODDM). What these educators wanted to know was, how could they reproduce these gains in their own school districts?

What they found at the root of the Outcomes Driven Developmental Model (ODDM) academic miracle of Johnson City were the ideas and practices of mastery learning. John R. Champlin, hired as superintendent in 1971, began the implementation of aspects of the mastery-learning model in one of the district's small elementary schools. Champlin credited his knowledge of mastery learning to a 1968 article written by Benjamin S. Bloom describing his Learning for Mastery model.[9] During the late 1960s Bloom designed an instructional process built upon the theoretical work of John B. Carroll. Bloom had been researching human variability in learning at the University of Chicago and was intrigued by Carroll's optimistic perspective on learner aptitude and his challenge of traditionally held notions regarding aptitude.[10]

Instead of conceiving of student aptitude as the *level* to which a student could learn a particular subject, Carroll maintained that student aptitude more accurately reflected an index of *learning rate*.[11] This implied that a student with a high aptitude for a subject would learn it more quickly, while one with low aptitude would learn it more slowly, but nonetheless, if the time were provided, the slower student would learn it.

Carroll argued that all children had the potential to learn well but differed in the amount of time each needed. He also identified factors that he believed influenced the time a child spent learning and the time he or she needed to learn. These factors included the learner characteristics of perservance, rate of learning, and ability to understand the instruction, and instructional characteristics such as the quality of instruction and the opportunity or needed time to learn.[12] The degree of student learning was determined in part by the amount of time a student needed to spend in learning, not strictly by the "ability" of the student. The complete model stated that the degree of student learning was a function of (1) the time allowed for instruction and (2) the perseverance of the student, divided by (3) the time needed for learning by the student, (4) the quality of the instruction given, and (5) the ability of the student to understand the instruction.

Using Carroll's conceptual framework, Bloom devised an outline for a mastery-learning strategy for the classroom. The strategy was designed so that the basic elements of instruction maximized the opportunities for the quality of instruction, the understanding of the instruction, and the time allowed for needed instruction.[13] Bloom's strategy included small units of learning, a sequence of formative testing for students, systematic correction of learning difficulties through improved instruction for students who did not learn the first time, and enrichment activities for students who mastered the unit learning quickly. Bloom maintained that if differential instruction was provided to different students when needed, "perhaps as many as 95 percent of students could achieve mastery of the predetermined level."[14]

The academic successes of mastery learning as a classroom strategy had been documented extensively throughout the 1970s.[15] However, the news on a systemwide implementation of mastery learning was not always positive. The Chicago city school district had abandoned its mandate for the implementation of mastery-learning reading programs in reaction to teacher resistance, the difficulty of implementing an individualized program for each student's learning rate, and uneven achievement gains.[16] By 1980 the Johnson City district became one of only a handful of school districts in the country that had been able to expand the strategies of mastery learning beyond the success of the classroom to districtwide implementation.

Educators involved in implementing and researching mastery learning sensed the need for a "vehicle whereby large-scale implementers might share their trials, tribulations, and insights" on mastery learning and the term given to its comprehensive implementation in a school district, i.e., outcome-based education. Champlin joined with several other educators to form a coalition of researchers and practioners who would work together on implementation strategies for outcome-based education and also spread the word on its effectiveness for student achievement.[17]

The coalition was named the Network of Outcome-Based Schools(NO-BS). "Its first task was to codify and elaborate the basic philosophical premises undergirding the various schools and districts in which mastery learning ideas were flourishing."[18] After this was accomplished, NO-BS became the major vehicle for the dissemination of outcome-based education. Its members traveled throughout the country promoting the educational model of OBE. As the one school district with the most comprehensive OBE reforms, Johnson City was showcased as the "prime example of the power and practicality of OBE."[19]

By 1989, four years after ODDM was validated and NO-BS was formed, the OBE movement was "growing rapidly, attracting hundreds of participants to OBE conferences featuring major figures in the OBE movement."[20] At one of these conferences in Minneapolis, Minnesota's state educational officials and legislators informally announced that the state would begin a comprehensive statewide effort to restructure Minnesota's schools through OBE. Efforts to implement OBE at the local level had now spread to statewide initiatives.

By the spring of 1991, the Outcomes Driven Developmental Model was described as a "gentle bulldozer" in *Quality Outcomes-Driven Education*, a journal published by a group of mastery-learning educators who had separated themselves from NO-BS to form the National Center for Outcome Based Education. The author explained his use of the metaphor in this way: "gentle" because "as a comprehensive school improvement process, it takes two to three years to implement all 20 of ODDM's components" and "bulldozer" because its "revolutionary spirit, from the beginning of adoption, bulldozes dysfunctional mind-sets, beliefs, and practices."[21]

A whirlwind was, perhaps, a better metaphor for the dissemination process of ODDM and outcome-based education, because one year later, school districts in nineteen states and in Canada had adopted ODDM as a conceptual model for the improvement of their instructional systems.[22] For those educators who were not able to visit Johnson City, attend an OBE conference, or hire one of the several consultancy groups that had formed around OBE, video journals were produced and available for subscription.[23] Outcome-based education had become a national movement and an educational business.

In 1992, Pennsylvania's became the first state board of education to reformulate its state curriculum along the guidelines of outcome-based education and to propose the adoption of fifty-three educational outcomes articulated by the educational department in all of its 501 school districts. However, this proposal met fierce political opposition from the conservative right, who feared the implications and classroom effects of the inclusion of student learning outcomes explicitly stating affective values.[24] They denounced OBE as "new age brainwashing." Ironically, segments of the same political constituency that had once endorsed the bottom-line academic indicators of OBE now lobbied state legislators to vote against the package of curriculum reform.

Not unlike the hybrid seeds developed for the "green revolution" of global agriculture during the 1960s, Johnson City's Outcomes Driven Developmental Model and other OBE models have been promulgated and planted in school districts and states across the nation by well-intentioned, ambitious, or panicked educational leaders during the past decade. This urgent transplanting of an educational model advertised to bear educational fruit in "two to three" years is more than an indication of America's need for bottom-line results and outcomes: it is a sign of America's impatient, historical search for educational "fixes."

Ever since early-nineteenth-century educational reformers extolled the virtues of common schooling for the political sustenance of our newly formed democratic republic, Americans have looked to its public schools as a "salvation" for all of its social ills and as a scapegoat for its failures.[25] American educators, frequently intoxicated by their own beliefs in the goodness of education for all, have likewise encouraged, sought, and promoted the expansion of schooling to meet the increasing social, political, and economic demands of the nation. In doing so, they have also accepted, albeit reluctantly, the burden of responsibility accompanying the public's demands.

Like their predecessors, 1980s educators responded quickly to the cries of the Chicken Littles in business, in government, and among the public that the American economic sky was falling and that the schools were to blame. Educational leaders ran about searching for ready answers and many found a promising solution in the ODDM model.

But have these educational fixes so eagerly applied in the past one hundred years of schooling changed the instructional programs of American schools? Larry Cuban sought the answer in his book, *How Teachers Taught: Constancy and Change in American Classrooms, 1880–1990*. Cuban asked why there is so little change in the overall uniformity of instructional practices in the American classroom over time and place, especially when educational leaders at the national, state, and district level regularly embrace and proudly display new programs that keep them "abreast of brand-new ideas in education" such as outcome-based education.[26]

In his extensive historical study of the "invulnerability of classrooms to change," Cuban found classrooms where change had taken place and was "alive and well," but he concluded that most efforts at "fundamental" reform, defined as reforms intended to "transform—alter permanently the structures of schooling," either failed or were changed themselves. If a reform managed to survive, it was most likely absorbed into the existing structure of the school as an "incremental" change.[27] An incremental change may improve the efficiency or effectiveness of schooling practices, but, as Cuban determined, it does not permanently alter the way schooling is done in the United States.

If schools are so "intractable to past efforts of reform,"[28] why did the changes initiated in Johnson City take hold and ultimately transform the instructional practices of the district? What conditions in the school and community of Johnson City allowed this fundamental reform to occur? And, lastly, will the efforts of the past decade to spread OBE throughout the nation cause fundamental change in other school districts?

1

Cui Bono?

"Cui bono?" means in Latin "to whose advantage?" or "who benefits?" as a determinant of the value or the motivation of an action. In the implementation and the evaluation of an educational change or reform, "cui bono?" becomes a central question for those effecting change, those affected by it, and those studying it. One may easily answer, "Of course, it's obvious, the children—the students—should benefit from school or any change in schooling. That's why we have schools, right?"

Certainly and simply, almost all efforts to improve schools have at their core an intention to benefit the children for whom schooling is based and to whom these efforts are directed. Age-graded classes, the organization of junior high schools, vocational education, life skills, whole language reading programs, social studies curricula, cooperative learning, and decentralized management are a few examples of the many reforms attempted or accomplished within schools during the past one hundred years with the primary intention to improve the learning of students.

But as vital as student learning is to the purpose of schooling, it is by no means the sole determinant or reason why we have schools. The state has social, political, and economic interests in the schooling of its youth, as do those individuals who are personally and financially invested in schooling, such as parents, community members, teachers, school administrators, and so forth. As each of these roles is considered, the analysis of "cui bono?" in schooling becomes increasingly complicated.

Nor does the benefit analysis of schooling become necessarily simpler by reducing the unit of size to that of the classroom. An instructional change implemented within a classroom may benefit only one group of students within the overall class while having no effect upon the other students or even having deleterious effects upon some students in the class. For example, learning to read by the phonic method has clear advantages for the auditory learner, but what effect does it have upon the visual or kinesthetic learner? The inclusion of exceptional children into the regular classroom has been proven to benefit the academic learning of these children, but what about the academic benefits for the other children?

Determining who actually benefits from schooling and educational change is a much more complex task than it first appears. The question, nonetheless, is of critical importance in the study of school reform in general and in the study of the Johnson City schools and community and of outcome-based education in particular. Since the first principle of ODDM and OBE states that "all children can learn," thereby establishing children and their learning outcomes as the foremost purpose of schooling, the analysis of both the intended and unintended consequences in efforts to achieve this goal is primary.

As defined by Spady, outcome-based education means using "clearly defined outcomes for all students" within the school's curriculum, measurement, and reporting systems; organizing instruction based upon the "performance capabilities and learning needs of students"; and modifying this instruction to enable all students to reach outcome goals, according to the results of "documented student learning."[1]

Similarly, the philosophical principles of Johnson City's ODDM state that "an essential function of schooling is to ensure that all students perform at high levels of learning and experience opportunities for individual success."[2] In both OBE and ODDM the student is identified as the major beneficiary of the outcomes. Increased student learning and success are defined as the primary outcomes.

But which student(s) will benefit from OBE? School learning in almost all situations involves groups of students rather than just one student. Within a class or group of students, how many will benefit from OBE? According to the principles of OBE and ODDM, *all* students will benefit. But what does this mean? Does it mean each student within the class—i.e., all—will demonstrate documented increases in achievement?

If the consequences of OBE match its intentions, then *all* students are expected to achieve an explicitly stated outcome goal; or as in ODDM, *all* students will perform at high levels. In each model, a verbal commitment is made to each student (and thus to all students) that a predetermined level of learning will be achieved by each and all.

Here again, one may easily add, "Of course, we want all students to learn and all to achieve at certain levels. We expect everyone to achieve in American schools." But, as we also know, many children in American schools fail subjects, grades, or courses; score below grade level on achievement tests; and finally drop out before graduation.

The extent of the failing, poor, or mediocre performances of American students has led critics of the American system to cry that our schools benefit only the top 20 to 30 percent of those children who enter the schoolhouse door.[3] They compare our weak showing with the performance of the Japanese who

> achieve their extremely high average level of academic performance by taking great care to see that their weakest students do well. As they have often claimed, they have "the best bottom 50 percent in the world" educationally—and virtually no dropouts.[4]

Proponents of OBE and ODDM make claims similar to those of the Japanese in that even the weakest students will achieve the expected outcomes. In making these claims, they challenge a fundamental belief within the American education system: the belief in the bell-shaped curve, the graphic representation of the distribution of random student intelligence and of achievement.[5] Instead of believing that student achievement will closely follow the bell-shaped curve of student aptitude or intelligence as measured by standardized tests, they propose that the amount of achievement can be increased for almost every student in defiance of his or her measured intelligence.

Educational psychologists who are proponents of the use of standardized tests to measure cognitive capacity and achievement hold that the visual representation of the statistical distribution of student cognitive aptitude and achievement will follow a normal probability curve or a bell-shaped curve when there is a uniform or "equal" opportunity to learn and a uniform or "equal" quality of instruction in a classroom of randomly assigned students.[6] According to the proponents of standardized tests often used by schools, such as the Wechsler Intelligence Scale for Children and California Achievement Test, the distribution of student aptitude or achievement scores will be documented by a bell-shaped curve with its highest point over a designated mean score.

However, OBE and ODDM advocates maintain that if the quality of instruction is adapted to the learner's needs, if the time needed to learn is provided, and if a student is motivated, *all* students are able to achieve to a certain level of knowledge and skill for each grade level. In the implementation of this reform, the student distribution of achievement on specified learning tasks can best be visualized, perhaps, as a vertical line of string hanging above that point or score that is considered mastery of the skill, knowledge, or task.

In the gradual reform of its entire system, grades K–12, the teachers, the administrators, the school board, and the parents of the Johnson City schools changed their beliefs about the so-called normal distribution of achievement among students as that represented by the bell-shaped curve.

To understand why and how these beliefs changed, and thereby facilitated the implementation of an instructional change with the possibility of benefiting all children, the work of Seymour Sarason is useful. In his book, *The Predictable Failure of Educational Reform*, Sarason states there are "two kinds of basic understandings or problems that should inform implementation" of educational change.[7]

The first of these two understandings is what Sarason loosely terms the *theoretical*, which is

> the weaving of a conceptual framework that makes sense of your ideas—that is, their interrelationships, the "real world" context from which they arose, their connections with the ideas and efforts of others, the different weights you assign to this or that factor. It is a framework in the present that has a past and a future direction.[8]

In Johnson City, ten years passed from the point of the initiation of an instructional practice in eight elementary classrooms that challenged traditional belief in the bell-shaped curve of student achievement to the unified, coherent articulation of the reform framework, which first appeared in 1982 and later became ODDM. The weaving of the conceptual framework underlying ODDM took time, as did the continuous process of making sense of the ideas and beliefs of superintendent and the central office staff, of the teachers, of the parents, and of the community as they meshed with each other, the "real world," and the "ideas and efforts of others."

The "ideas and efforts of others," the research that undergirded Johnson City's instructional change, originated in Bloom's Learning for Mastery model.[9] If, when needed, differential instruction was provided to students, then almost all students could achieve mastery of the predetermined level. Only those students who were unwilling and refused to learn would not achieve mastery, and they possibly could become motivated through programs directed at motivation. In effect, the implementation of the mastery learning strategy in a classroom could push to the right the achievement of 95 per cent of the students in the bell-shaped curve of the random distribution of "ability," boosting almost all to attainment of the task, knowledge, or skill.

Mastery learning promised that a huge portion of students who under traditional school circumstances had mediocre, poor, and even failing grades, could, with enough time and quality instruction, achieve at the "B" and "A" level. It maintained that under the right conditions, almost *all* students could learn and achieve at mastery levels.

Ideally, Americans may want this for all students in our schools. Where it becomes problematic is in the public and personal investment of the financial resources to provide "enough time and quality instruction" for this to occur and in our ideological commitment to a meritocratic and competitive society where there are striking variations in the socioeconomic status of different segments of the American population. Assuming that each student will persevere in the effort needed to learn, the amount and cost of resources to be invested in the process are not established or described in this model. But, even if money were not a salient issue in schooling, are we, as Americans who live in a competitively structured society, really prepared to allow students from every socioeconomic station to achieve mastery at the "A" or "B" level? Do we really believe that *all* students should be guaranteed to benefit to an established level in American schooling and society?

Several underlying factors predisposed the Johnson City schools in the 1960s and 1970s to support programs that proposed to lift the bulk of its students to high levels of achievement, providing a receptive environment in which this "theoretical" change could take root.

The reasons for its appeal to many within the Johnson City schools and community can be sought in Sarason's second explanation of what is necessary to inform the implementation of educational change. Sarason terms this the *social-institutional context*, i.e., the

structure, implicit and explicit rules, traditions, power relationships, and purposes variously defined by its members. It is
dynamic in that it is characterized by continuous activity and
interchanges both within its boundaries and between it and its
community surround. It is a context that can be described, but it
is not a context that can be understood by what we ordinarily
mean by description. It has covert as well as overt features.[10]

Sarason warns that only by understanding this context is it possible to implement changes that will result in replication of an educational reform rather than in superficial imitation, which he calls
"sloganeering and advertising, an imitation of surface phenomena
devoid of substance."[11] Only by carefully investigating the subtle
interrelationships of the "theoretical" and the "social-institutional context" of the school and community are we able to determine what
knowledge, beliefs, values, and relationships of both the schools and
community of Johnson City permitted the planting of a change that
benefited the bulk of its students and pushed them to the right of the
midpoint of the bell-shaped curve.

Refining Sarason's description of the social-institutional context
further, Cuban delineates two overlapping contexts within the social-
institutional context that shape an instructional change. Cuban first
describes the outer context, consisting of the "long-term cultural
beliefs about the nature of knowledge, what teaching and learning
should be, and the ethnic, racial, and social backgrounds of the children attending the school."[12] This mixes with the second inner context
of "teacher beliefs and occupational ethos" to influence the form of a
change in schooling, and determines whether it will become a fundamental or incremental change.

The social-institutional context with its overlapping layers is designated by Gerald Grant in *The World We Created at Hamilton High
School* as the family mix and "the cultural ground." Grant defines the
"cultural ground" as

the deep ground influencing the forms of socialization in the family and attitudes toward schooling. Patterns of culture shape the
actions of teachers and school officials, enhancing some policies
and frustrating others. We are seldom aware of how much our culture has taught us until we leave it.[13]

Here, in this context, in the cultural ground of the knowledge,
beliefs, and values of the children, the staff, and the community of

Johnson City, we begin to understand why this conceptual framework of mastery learning took hold so firmly and comprehensively, and to understand what may be necessary to replicate such an instructional change in other schools and communities. As we fold back the outer layers of schooling, we find the stuff that comprises the cultural ground of Johnson City and how this stuff has been shaped by the corporate ethos of the Endicott Johnson Corporation and International Business Machines, the two major economic forces in this community and area. Each corporation, although very different in the type of product it manufactured and the type of worker it employed, exerted far more than an economic influence upon the values of this community. Each corporation shaped the social and political values of the community and formed the basis for the instructional changes that promised to benefit all, rather than some, of its students.

2

The Endicott Johnson Ethos

To understand why an instructional strategy like mastery learning with its promise of a broad expansion of achievement benefits to all students took root in the Johnson City schools, one must probe the long-held cultural beliefs and patterns of both the schools and community. Forming the outer layer of the social-institutional context, these deep-rooted cultural beliefs are those unspoken habits and assumptions that silently guide the everyday movements of a school and community. They can often be sensed when someone in the school or community is asked why things are done this way or that, and the reply is, "Well, that's just the way we do things around here. It's been this way as long as I can remember. Doesn't everybody do it this way?"

This seemingly "natural" way of doing things may only rise above the smooth surface of community life when a citizen leaves his or her own community or when an outsider visits the community. These cultural patterns gently shade and blend overt decisions into habits forming the ethos of a school or a community, what Grant calls "the sharing of attitudes, values, and beliefs that bond disparate individuals into a community."[1]

The ethos shaped by ODDM and the Johnson City schools emphasizes universal inclusivity and benefit to students. In ODDM educational resources are managed so that almost all students, even mildly handicapped and some severely handicapped children, are the beneficiaries. Although two decades of school reform led to the

19

articulation of the belief statement of ODDM that "all students will learn well," its source lay in the taproots of the economic history and ethos of the community. The rich, deep ground of this history and ethos, described and analyzed in this chapter, was shaped by the labor and management practices of the Endicott Johnson Shoe Corporation (EJ), and of its patriarch, "George F." Johnson.

"Which way EJ?"

Johnson City, New York, was Ida Tarbell's first stop in her investigation of the Endicott Johnson Corporation in 1919. A leading muckraker intent on uncovering dishonesty in American corporations, Tarbell was surprised to find that the small urban village nestled west of the city of Binghamton had recently changed its name to honor the man she had come to expose. Originally Lestershire, the town had been renamed Johnson City for the corporation's president, George F. Johnson. Although Johnson himself was curiously missing during her visit, Tarbell wrote that she was unable to "escape him" from the moment she passed under the huge cast concrete arch leading into Johnson City.[2]

The arch proclaimed the two shoe towns of Endicott and Johnson City to be the "Home of the Square Deal." A large boulder on the side of the road explained that the arch was "Erected by the E-J Workers in Honor of George F. Johnson in Appreciation of the Square Deal Policy, May 1, A.D. 1919." Wherever Tarbell went in the towns and in the factories, whether talking to managers or employees, men or women, native or foreign-born, she found that George F. "was so persistently and so insistently quoted, so built into the minds and habits of the establishment that you don't need to see him to know him."[3] She became determined to find out just how George F. had made such an indelible mark upon the people of these towns.

George Francis Johnson, born in 1857, began working at the age of thirteen in the shoe trade, first stripping leather from old boots until he worked his way up to the position of foreman with the Lester Boot Factory in Binghamton, New York, in 1882. Six years later, in 1888, Johnson as an assistant superintendent was appointed to oversee the construction of a factory two miles west of Binghamton that was to be surrounded by a model community named Lestershire. In this model community, the shoe company would provide workers with the "benefits and guidance of a middle class life."[4] By 1899, Johnson had bought half interest in the firm from a new owner named Endicott, and the new firm, Endicott, Johnson & Company, was created.

With the help of his brothers Harry L. and C. Fred, Johnson expanded the capabilities and profits of the shoe-manufacturing operation such that employment rose from two thousand workers in 1901 to thirteen thousand workers by 1919. In addition to dramatically increasing production, profits, and employment, Johnson organized the factories as a vertical corporation in which all aspects of production from the tanning of the raw leather to the boxing of the shoes was done in the Endicott Johnson factories. He also opened his own retail stores to market the corporation's products.

In these same two decades of astounding business success, Johnson formulated and implemented an ethos of a "co-operative commonwealth" of business and community that turned his shoe towns into model communities of industrial harmony. This benevolent partnership between capital and labor attracted the attention of national figures like Tarbell and had lasting effects upon the complex interrelationships of community, schooling, and the dominant economic ethos.

In his own prolific writings, Johnson attributed the success and harmony of the EJ communities to his strong but simple belief in the Golden Rule, the goodness of men, and the inextricable relationship of labor and capital. His own phrase for the Golden Rule was the "square deal," which meant "putting yourself in the other fellow's place . . . trying to get the other fellow's point of view."[5] His faith that "90% of humans were good" directed that the business run upon "the confidence we have in the 90 percent, rather than on the suspicion we have of the 10 percent."[6] And remembering his early days as a shoe laborer, Johnson valued labor as the more important contributor in the partnership of labor and capital:

> It is sometimes said that laboring people are more dependent upon capital than capital upon labor. This is a grave mistake. . . . Labor can live, labor can produce, and reproduce. . . . But capital is a weak and helpless thing, without brains or muscle . . . until put to work by labor, and made useful—as a joint partner of labor—in producing those things which the world is ready to buy.[7]

Johnson's vision for this partnership of labor and capital was clearly and succinctly spelled out in a small booklet given to new workers in the early 1920s, titled "An E-J Worker's First Lesson in the Square Deal." The pamphlet promised fair treatment and security for the worker and his or her family as part of "the Endicott Johnson happy family." "In fair return" for the good wages and benefits, the worker would make "an honest effort to do the work well" and would do "a fair and sufficient amount of it."[8]

As a member of the "Endicott-Johnson family," a worker was entitled to benefits still untested in many American industries and unheard of in many of the countries from which a substantial number of EJ employed workers had emigrated. Johnson viewed these benefits as evidence of his own personal belief system and his commitment to the 90 percent of his workers who were good human beings and who were expected to corral the shirking behavior of the remaining 10 percent.[9]

Johnson's paternalistic and pragmatic labor policies were strongly connected to the development of American welfare capitalism and to the progressive social movements of the early twentieth century. Corporate responsibility for some portion of the welfare of its workers was found in as many as two thousand American companies by 1917.[10]

The social and financial climate of his era and his own personal history combined with Johnson's shrewd understanding of shoemaking and industrial organization. The corporate paternalism he coined "The EJ happy family" provided a secure and stable relationship for both labor and management. Johnson's use of the metaphor of family reinforced the simple but pervasive ideal of caring, belonging, and loyalty for all members in a closely knit, socially cohesive unit. No altruistic dreamer, Johnson deluded neither himself nor his workers about the reciprocal nature of those benefits he extended to his workers. In his letters and company publications, he acknowledged frankly the important contribution happy, satisfied workers made to a financially successful business.

Endicott Johnson's benefits included a company-financed mortgage on a company-built home; medical, dental, and legal services; a flexible, eight-hour day; company cafeterias and markets; a profit-sharing plan; pensions; and a community fire company and police services. Company recreational, athletic, and educational facilities such as a golf course, swimming pools, ball fields, carousels, and libraries were open to all in the community whether one worked for Endicott Johnson or not. Everyone received a free pair of shoes at Christmas and on birthdays, even the inmates of the town jail.

The tales of the jobs and prosperous communities created by the Endicott Johnson Corporation easily caught the attention of the tens of thousands of eastern and southern European immigrants who were lured to America by dreams of democracy and a full stomach. These tales of a secure and happy life in Johnson City and its sister shoe town, Endicott, also swayed the heads of nearby Pennsylvanians struggling in the anthracite coal mines. "Which way E.J.?" was a common question asked on Ellis Island, New York, and in Scranton, Pennsylvania, as newcomers and natives tried to find the railroad tracks that led to Binghamton, New York—so they could follow them on foot.

By the early 1920s, one third of EJ's workers were foreign-born. Johnson welcomed these immigrants, calling them the "New Americans" and urged the native-born workers to accept them into the "great family of E.J. Workers." He encouraged his workers to play fair with their "foreign born associate . . . to have patience with him when he talks to you in broken language . . . help him form his sentences correctly."[11] He chastised local officials and citizens for their unfair discrimination toward the incoming immigrants and reminded them that they "have the same rights to buy properties where they choose as have others." He took a strong stand against the Ku Klux Klan, which had begun to organize in southern New York against the onslaught of Catholic immigrants.[12]

Johnson also encouraged and supported the hiring of both single and married women. He consistently maintained the practice into the Great Depression in spite of criticism expressed by both men and women in letters to the editors of local papers. Such letters censured married working women for not giving up their jobs to unemployed men.[13] Johnson put the local debate to an end by publishing a letter that strongly stated that "Any person who is willing to work ought to be able to find work . . . it certainly is most unfair to consider discharging a woman just because she is 'married.' It would be just as unfair to discharge a woman because she was not married."[14]

The long, caring arms of the Endicott Johnson Corporation extended well beyond the boundaries of the factory yards to the outer community. EJ generosity provided for new schools, some of which were named after Johnson's family members. Johnson's support of education, however, was limited to public schools, as noted in this letter to a priest who asked for his help:

> I deprecate and deplore any effort which separates our children
> into groups of any kind. I believe the public school of the United

States has done more to break down prejudice, hatred, and unkind thought than any one single institution in our nation.[15]

Johnson's financial support for public education also ended with high school graduation. He saw very little need for a college education, especially when good jobs and wages were waiting for graduates in his shoe factories and offices. Each year he visited the high schools of both towns and spoke to the young adults about the virtues of life and their future with the Endicott Johnson Corporation. College might be necessary for a small percentage of the youth who aspired to be lawyers, doctors, or ministers, Johnson conceded, but otherwise it was a waste of time and money:

> I haven't anything against colleges. Far from it. But if I had a boy that I wanted to make a tanner or a shoe manufacturer, I wouldn't send him to college. I would figure that I was throwing away five of the most valuable years that he possibly could have in the factory or tannery. . . . And so I say to shoemakers. The chances are your children will make better tanners and shoemakers than they will college professors, lawyers, preachers, etc.[16]

Johnson and Endicott Johnson were "family" for the workers and towns of Johnson City and Endicott. The Square Deal provided an idyllic "middle class" for EJ workers. In exchange, however, the shoeworker was required to be content with the monotony of factory work, to accept a narrow choice of occupation, to tolerate a lower wage scale compared to other types of manufacturing work, and above all, to spurn the advances of the labor organizers who visited the community time and again.

No Unions, No "Evil Teachers"

Despite his earlier radical days in the shoe trade, George F. Johnson could not and would not abide labor unions. As a result, union organizers made few inroads in organizing the shops of the Endicott Johnson factories from the early 1900s through the 1930s. Although he did employ members of the Boot and Shoemakers Union, Johnson felt that the workers in his factories, with their many benefits, had no need for unions. To track any union infiltration, he hired undercover "spies" and admitted freely his benevolent labor practices were designed to foil the unions and "Bolshevism."

During the financially difficult years of the Depression, the Johnson family appealed repeatedly to the loyalty of its workers to hold fast against unionism, as seen in this quote from the Johnson-owned *Binghamton Sun* newspaper:

> You may be certain IT IS NOT FOR YOUR SAKE that strangers come into the community, circulate their "vile propaganda," seeking to create discontent and unhappiness and THEN DISAPPEAR, to work in SOME OTHER FIELD. Pay no attention to EVIL TEACHERS, false doctrines and UNHEALTHY PROPAGANDA.[17]

They reminded workers of how well they were faring in comparison to workers (one out of four nationwide) who had lost their jobs and stood in line for bread and soup during the worst years of the Depression.

In the 1940 union election, as in past elections, EJ workers strongly saluted the economic paternalism of EJ by soundly defeating the threat of the union organization of the Endicott Johnson shoe factory workers.

The onset of World War II and the subsequent demand for boots for American G.I.s pulled the company out of the financial uncertainties of the late 1930s and restored the glow of prosperity to both the firm and the community. The orders for EJ's heavy shoes skyrocketed. The firm's only major problem was a labor shortage due to the enlisting of many shoe workers into the armed forces.

The death of George F. Johnson in 1948 was felt throughout the corporation and boded ill. Confronted with cheaper foreign imports, higher local labor costs, and growing state taxes, the second generation of Johnsons, in full control of the factories in the 1950s, began building plants where the labor was cheaper, such as Pennsylvania, Mississippi, and Puerto Rico. EJ's acclaimed commitment to the partnership of labor and capital eroded along with its loyalty to the communities of New York's Southern Tier.

Still, the demands of the Korean War helped to keep local employment figures between seventeen and eighteen thousand in the early 1950s. With the war's end, however, Endicott Johnson found itself unable to rebound and recapture a consumer market demanding a lighter, more stylish pair of shoes. Foreign competition continued to bite deeper into United States shoe production. Several financial crises spurred by poor management decisions threatened the mighty

Endicott Johnson Shoe Company in the late 1950s. The steady EJ grip upon the wheel of the life and culture of Johnson City began to loosen.

In 1919 Tarbell had ended her article on George F. and EJ by wondering, "Will it endure?" Answering her own question, she stated,

> [It will] So long as endures the wisdom at the top which insists that if you would lead them into ways of peaceful labor you must be one of them. Understanding of the Square Deal is not vouchsafed to the absent capitalist. It is the precious knowledge of him who has learned the joy and the value of neighborliness and lives with those whom he would lead.[18]

The value of neighborliness was firmly entrenched in the beliefs of George F. Johnson. Just as he insisted that he and his family live and work in the factories and towns he and Endicott Johnson created, he spun an ethos of "one for all, and all for one," of an inclusive community steeped in a tradition of social responsibility.

The Self, Others, and Work

As the Korean War ended in a stalemate in 1953, the era of the cooperative commonwealth of George F. Johnson and the Endicott Johnson Corporation was crumbling in the path of a juggernaut of international competition. To residents of Johnson City, the new era was represented in the international economic success of International Business Machines (IBM) and the social status a job at IBM brought to its workers. As the one era made way for the next, the residents of the community of Johnson City began, knowingly and unknowingly, to reshape themselves and their pasts to form their identities for the future.

In the analysis of this transition, questions arise regarding the meaning of the self within a community and expose the dilemma of the self-reliant self as opposed to the self in community—the self-sufficient part as opposed to the interdependent whole.

In *Habits of the Heart*, Bellah and his coauthors state that "the tension between self-reliant competitive enterprise and a sense of public solidarity espoused by civic republicans has been the most important unresolved problem in American history."[19] In their analysis of the meaning of the public good within the past hundred years of American history, they find a persistent American cultural "ambivalence about the meshing of self-reliance and community" and a historical "ambivalence over the question of how to combine individual autonomy and the interrelationships of a complex modern economy."[20]

Until the late 1950s, the meaning of the self, the meaning of the self with others in family, in groups, and in community, and the meaning of the self and one's work or occupation in Johnson City were inextricably interwoven with the dominant social and economic ethos of Endicott Johnson. As such, a secure, harmonious balance of the self and others (the social) and the self and work (the economic) existed within a well-defined community of mutual interest. This reciprocity of interest, the common good, the "cooperative commonwealth," was based upon Johnson's beliefs in the partnership of labor and capital, the goodness of the "90 percent," and the Golden Rule.

In Johnson's partnership of capital and labor, the interdependent relationship permitted no exclusionary, competing relationships outside of the "EJ family." Management and capital were not permitted to profiteer by isolating portions of wealth for their self-interest or by investing these portions in outside interests unrelated to the overall health of both the economic and social enterprises *within* the EJ community. Likewise, labor was not permitted to organize into unions separately from this partnership but was enticed through benefits to affirm the cooperative relationship in an ongoing identification with the mutual interests of capital.

The relationship between both was voluntary and private, and therefore resided within the tenets of free enterprise of American economic capitalism in the late nineteenth and early twentieth centuries. The partnership, however, did not embrace capitalism's freewheeling emphasis upon either the unrestrained drive of individual self-interest and economic competition promoted by the theories of Adam Smith or upon the theory of natural selection and the social competitiveness promulgated by the Darwinists of Johnson's time.

Johnson's own brand of economic theory was probably influenced by the writings of the Welsh political economist, Robert Owen. Owen argued that human identity was crucially involved with an individual's participation in family, community, and occupational groups.[21] In his *His New View of Society* or *Essays on the Principle of the Formation of the Human Character*, published in the year of Johnson's birth, Owen advocated the operation of economically and socially interdependent collectives or communities.

In such communities, social and economic interests were rationally intertwined and mutually supportive. Within a benevolent, socially nurturing network of an economically functioning and viable community, Owen believed, ignorance, crime, and poverty could be eliminated through the social formation of individual character by collective, economically profitable enterprise and a common education. He firmly maintained that when a "man's desire of self-happiness" was directed through rational instruction by "true knowledge," his actions would be "virtuous and beneficial."

In communities like New Lanark Mills, Scotland, and New Harmony, Indiana, in which Owen had financially invested, "every individual will necessarily endeavor to promote the happiness of every other individual within his sphere of action; because he must clearly . . . comprehend such conduct to be the essence of self-interest."[22] In his writings and public addresses, Owen strongly lobbied both the British Crown and business interests in Great Britain and the United States for the development of benevolent, capitalist communities with provisions of public schooling and character training within each community. Johnson appears to have interpreted this as common schooling that prepared a child with education and character training for everyday life and factory work.

In addition to this probable connection with Owen's work, the extensive writings of George F. Johnson and the ethos he established in the EJ factories and communities reflected the strong religious influence of his Methodist mother and indicated a spiritual devotion to the pursuit of virtue that lay beyond the rational quest for knowledge, wisdom, and mutual self-interest in Owen's treatises. Johnson's own form of welfare capitalism included an unwavering faith in the goodness of men and a penchant for the pursuit of virtue in daily private and public life. His firm belief in his own statement that "90 percent of humans are good"[23] as well as his insistence that EJ benefits should extend to all in the community—employed by EJ or not, in jail or just visiting—are examples of this. Above his desk hung a plaque containing this biblical passage from Gal. 6:9, "And let us not weary in well-doing, for in due season we shall reap, if we do not lose heart."

The quest for American democratic republicanism in the nineteenth century may also have affected Johnson's emphasis on the importance of virtue in individual and social life. The notion of virtue had weighed heavily upon the minds of such framers of the Constitution as James Madison as they articulated the framework for the "public good" within a democratic republic.[24] Within the late eighteenth and nineteenth centuries, virtue was described as an "ideal of character" that "depended upon the belief that besides the grimly self-focused passions, there was in human beings a capacity to apprehend and pursue the good and to recognize in the character of others the qualities of integrity, grace, and excellence."[25] The pursuit of virtue was inherently more than a reciprocity of self-interests, of one hand washing the other. To live the virtuous life implied a human capacity to pursue the "good" within oneself and in others in one's effort to be rewarded with a spiritual state of grace.

Contemporaries of Johnson such as the industrialist Andrew Carnegie and the socialist Eugene Debs held radically different views as to the role of government in the affairs of its citizens. But each believed that the paradoxical nature of the freedom of the self versus the shared support and constraint of community in an emerging industrial and corporate economic society had to be confined within a public moral order that defined "just" institutions and "virtuous" citizens.[26] Within this era, for the established capitalist, the egalitarian populist, or the pragmatic progressive, "work, welfare, and authority . . . [were] tightly interrelated and embedded in community life" and in the mutual understanding and pursuit of justice and virtue.[27]

In this cultural milieu of mores stressing the virtues of community, Johnson City had been forged as a model "middle-class" community of inclusivity and universal benefit. The industrial ethos of Endicott Johnson and George F. Johnson, based on doing good for all, strongly resembles the belief underlying mastery learning and ODDM in which all children can learn and achieve at high levels, where all can accrue the benefits of schooling. In a hypothetical conceptualization of the bell-shaped curve of the human capacity for goodness and for work, George F. maintained that "90 percent of humans" were to the right of midpoint. His belief in the human capacity to work is similar to that of mastery learning's assumption about students' capacity to achieve. Both beliefs value human effort or perseverance as an integral aspect of achievement, understate the significance of aptitude, and grant the individual the time needed to work or achieve the task. They both resemble the Japanese belief that student achievement is based upon effort, not talent as stressed in the United States.[28] Within each is the belief that regardless of inherited aptitude, the possibility exists for a person to achieve at certain levels of mastery if the time is provided and the human desire is nurtured.

But by the 1960s, a changing world was pulling at Johnson City's webs of social and economic interdependence and began to strangle the health of the community. Residents recognized the need for self-reliance and independence but wondered what would be sacrificed in their efforts to free themselves from the dominant economic interests of EJ. Was it possible to release themselves from their economic dependence upon EJ and still keep intact the social networks fostered by EJ? Or, would the financial difficulties of EJ lead to the gradual social disintegration of the community and to a new era based upon the interests of "some" rather than "all"?

Endicott Johnson engendered an ethos of human effort and universal benefit within a community. But as the next chapter reveals, this belief was not sufficient to compel a new school board into building the foundation for instructional changes that also championed this belief. Other social and economic factors and beliefs within the community would also be necessary to root these changes in the school system.

3

Community Disequilibrium

As immigrants found jobs in the shoe factories and settled into the communities of Johnson City and Endicott, they started families. When their children entered school, they cautioned them "to behave, to stay out of trouble," so that a job in the shoe factories would be waiting for them when they graduated from the Johnson City High School. But the EJ children discovered as they progressed through the grades that the words used to guide their lives were not the same for all the boys and girls in their classes. Some of the other children, those who lived south of Main Street, were told by their parents to "be" doctors, lawyers, or engineers at IBM. These children talked about going to college. These children were not called "hunkies" or "roundheads" by the teachers, nor were they scolded because they smelled of garlic. When they reached ninth grade, these others were placed in the college-bound section, while the children of EJ parents were advised "to forget the academic courses." They were told, "Your parents are EJers; you will be, too."[1]

Only later, after some of the EJ boys returned to Johnson City after serving in the military in the Korean War, did they recognize the patterns of their early lives. Coming home with new skills and perspectives on life, they realized how the schools had sorted them and their classmates into their adult roles according to their parents' occupations and that they no longer fit these roles. They did not want to labor on the hot factory floors of EJ as their parents had. They, too, wanted to "be." They also found a changing Johnson City.

31

Endicott Johnson, the former corporate giant and dominant employer in Broome County, was losing control of the national shoe market to foreign competition and had been economically dwarfed by the global conglomerate IBM, located in nearby Endicott. The economic decline of EJ spelled the end of the company-financed mortgages, community dinners, and Sunday ball games, and the closing of the community swimming pool and company cafeterias. Only one of the George F. Johnson's free carousels—built so that no child in the two towns would be denied a ride, as George had been as a little boy without a nickel—was still operating. For nearly sixty years, the benevolent capitalism of the Endicott Johnson Corporation had provided a wealth of social benefits and created a middle-class community for working-class shoe workers whose low wages could not have supported such a lifestyle. But as one EJ benefit after another benefit stopped, the path to a middle-class life no longer wound through Endicott Johnson, nor were some of its characteristics guaranteed with community membership. The young people of Johnson City slowly began to realize that each one as an individual would have to find his or her own way without EJ. Getting into the IBM plant at Endicott was the new ticket, but getting a job at IBM was not easy. One needed a personal contact, sufficient education, and the right look to get into IBM. As they drove past the members-only IBM country club and golf course on their way to Endicott, they wondered if they had what was needed to be a member of the IBM elite.

The IBM Way

In 1955, when IBM's founder Thomas J. Watson Sr. retired, IBM was the world's largest nonunion corporation. That year the technological behemoth earned $696,294,000. To many in the United States and across the world, IBM symbolized technologically advanced products and elite, white-collar employment.[2]

International Business Machines had its beginning in 1914 in the formation of a holding company for several small firms, including one in Endicott called the International Time Recording Company (ITR), a manufacturer of time clocks. At the urging of the financier that had managed the merger of these firms into the Computing-Tabulating-Recording Company (CTR), the new board of directors hired Thomas Watson Sr. as their chief operating officer.

Watson had grown up in the Southern Tier region of New York

about seventy miles from Johnson City and had traveled the area as a salesman for National Cash Register (NCR). After twenty years of work and successfully rising to the top of NCR's management, he had been fired by its eccentric president. Although unemployed at the age of forty, Watson had lost neither his self-confidence nor his bravado. He sensed the future importance of the small firms' potential market, especially the Tabulating Machine Company, the New Jersey brainchild of Herman Hollerith; it was a company that manufactured machines capable of tabulating massive amounts of data. After convincing the CTR board to hire him, Watson proposed a modest salary, but wanted a substantial part of the future earnings of the holding company.[3] The board agreed. By 1923, Watson had tripled the size of CTR, its sales, and its dividends. In 1924 he was named the chief executive officer of CTR and proclaimed his hopes for the corporation's worldwide future by changing its name to International Business Machines.

Impressed by the loyalty, low wages, and aversion to unions of the workers of Endicott and Johnson City that had been instilled by George F. Johnson, Watson decided to make the area the factory home of IBM.[4] Over the next thirty years, Watson forged the firm's interests and identity into a corporation known around the world. It had installations in 105 nations and was worth 170 times its base in 1914. Upon his retirement in 1956, Watson turned the reins of this corporation of awesome size, wealth, and influence over to his son, Thomas J. Watson Jr.

During the 1950s, as Endicott Johnson was groaning under the threat of foreign competition, IBM was surging ahead and exerting its dominance of the world's technological market. A Johnson City resident did not need to read the financial papers to know of the fortunes of these two corporations; they were the daily talk in Main Street diners and over Johnson City dinner tables.

EJ and IBM, George F. Johnson and Thomas J. Watson Sr.: two corporations and two leaders who so shaped the life of the communities in the northern Susquehanna Valley of New York during the first six decades of the twentieth century that their creations and accomplishments formed the fiber of the collective unconscious of all who lived, worked, and played there. How people perceived the communities of Endicott and Johnson City, how they perceived those who worked for each firm, and how they perceived themselves were directly influenced by their relationships with one of the two firms. Both Watson and Johnson were emblematic of a time in American history when corporate giants individually crafted the vision and identity of a corporation. Although each emblazoned a seal upon his business and employees that was indelibly his own, the cultures of the two nearby corporations overlapped each other; they shared some characteristics but also had glaring differences.

Both Johnson and Watson came from humble beginnings and grew up without the benefit of any advanced education. Both worked their way into established companies and boldly convinced wealthier interests to finance their ideas. They brought a spiritual, almost religious, commitment to their firms, a commitment expected from all who worked for them. Like Johnson, Watson constantly pressed his vision and philosophy upon his employees through company publications, slogans such as "Think," and company songs. Watson added the company retreat to Johnson's forms of spirited corporate indoctrination. While at National Cash Register, Watson had learned from his former boss the psychological value of company-sponsored retreats for his top-producing salesmen. Reserved for those who achieved 100 percent of their sales quotas, IBM retreats were like religious revival meetings in their intensity. Endless sales presentations and boisterous songs accompanied sumptuous food and often spartan accommodations. Watson claimed that

> You cannot be a success in any business without believing that it
> is the greatest business in the world. . . . You have to put your heart
> in the business and the business in your heart.[5]

Just as Johnson had urged his workers to sign loyalty oaths to him and EJ and to spurn the lure of unions, Watson enjoined his men to have blind loyalty to IBM:

> If you are loyal you are successful. . . . The man who is loyal to his
> work is not wrung nor perplexed by doubts, he sticks to the ship,
> and if the ship founders, he goes down like a hero with colors fly-
> ing at the masthead and the band playing.[6]

For both EJ and IBM, such loyalty was being part of the corporate family, a metaphor both men used effectively time and again in their voluminous communications to employees. The reciprocal bond between manager and employee had benefits for both; in return for this loyalty, each corporation extended generous benefits to its workers and families. Johnson called his bond with his employees the "Square Deal"; Watson named his "The Golden Rule."

As the adored patriarchs of their communities, both men enjoyed the worship of community residents as well as national and international renown. When Johnson returned home after wintering in Florida, schools and factories closed so all residents could gather and greet George F. in his motorcade through the town's streets. The residents of Endicott and Johnson City also followed the news of Watson closely and regarded him with awe and admiration, even if they were not encouraged to mingle so closely with this captain of industry as they were with Johnson. Both men personified the benevolent capitalist who provided for the welfare of his employees and created a corporate ethos that wrapped around each employee and spread throughout the community.

But profound differences did separate the two men, their visions, and their corporations. Each identified with the interests of a different social class and those aspects of life that construct the meaning of social class, such as the use of money and leisure time, personal habits, education, and one's relationship with one's community.

Endicott Johnson manufactured and sold shoes, mostly workingman's shoes. The manufacture of shoes was a workingman's employment, a skilled trade, a blue-collar job. Johnson never once forgot from whence he had come and clearly celebrated the honest toil of manual labor. Most at home with the common man, his labor, and his pleasures, Johnson was uncomfortable with what he viewed as the encumbering luxuries of financial success, and during disputes was more apt to take the side of the workingman over the established authorities within the community. He despised the "vulgar rich" and their offensive means of spending money on such useless things as mausoleums. He was quick to take up the cudgels for that weekly recreation of the factory worker, the Sunday baseball game and the quaffing of beer that accompanied the sport. Although a very religious man, Johnson used his influence over local disapproving church leaders to permit this workingman's recreation. Johnson wrote

> I have never known any good to be accomplished by the efforts of ministers of the Gospel to clean up cities, municipalities or communities—to close moving pictures, or to enforce prohibition, or to interfere with Sunday recreation. . . . every time we treat a human being decently and fairly we are practicing religion—real practical religion.[7]

In contrast, Watson wanted not a sniff nor sign of manual labor about his employees. Watson was famous for his stiff white collar, striped tie, dark suit, and impeccable grooming, an attire he expected for each IBM employee from the lowliest repairman to the top executive. According to Watson,

> We meet people for the first time, and they judge the company by our appearance. The man who wishes to be a success in business must dress the part.

Presentation of self and presentation to one's customers were personal and social skills highly valued by Watson. He wanted his employees to be more than salesmen; he wanted them to be professionals who would educate their customers about the needs of their businesses. Therefore, Watson stressed the importance of education. Unlike Johnson, who denigrated higher education and extolled the virtues of manual labor, Watson encouraged his employees to continue their schooling at the expense of the company. By the beginning of World War II, 70 percent of the IBM's employees had enrolled in one of more courses in IBM's educational programs. By 1969, over 50 percent were college graduates.[9] In contrast, Johnson believed that "the only producer and the only people who make wealth are those who labor."[10] Watson believed that wealth could be created through ideas, education, and service to one's customers.

These contrasting conceptions of the creation of wealth and the role of education in this process profoundly influenced the curriculum and programs of the Johnson City school district and the adult lives of the district's students. The Endicott Johnson ethos had held sway over the lives of Johnson City residents, shaping their aspirations and occupations. Beginning in the 1960s, Watson and IBM's emphasis upon the value of continued education would change the course of the Johnson City schools.

Watson thrived upon pomp and circumstance and sought the luxuries that spelled success in the eyes of the world. To establish the IBM man as a cut above the rest, Watson created a persona of prestige and elitism for the IBM man and his social station in life. None of his rewards for his employees worked as well as the creation of private country clubs and golf courses in developing the refined, exclusive esprit de corps that went with a job at IBM. As Belden and Belden stated in their biography of Watson, the country club "symbolized the company spirit of IBM . . . [it was] the embodiment of their community of interests and their sense of being the Elect."[11]

For Watson and for IBM, being the elect was of supreme importance. In this way, an IBM man impressed his customers; he was not
merely the seller of services or wares; he sold himself and he sold IBM.
He communicated that employment at IBM was not for everyone but
only for the best, primarily for that white male who fit the IBM image
and, of course, followed Watson's dictates to the letter. According to
Rodgers,

> It was almost exclusively a male world at IBM, except for certain
> factory jobs, clinic nurses, and some typists. Male secretaries were
> the rule until World War II compelled a change in policy. Prior to
> the war, employees were overwhelmingly male and Protestant.
> The message to personnel interviewers evoked no less response
> by reason of the fact that it was oblique, unwritten, and theoreti-
> cally unoffical. Watson liked the kind of men who were calm,
> polite, devoted, and subjugated editions of himself, whose ambi-
> tion found expression in a total involvement in their jobs, leaders
> who were enthusiastically content to be followers. They were an
> industrial ethnic group, nationalists of the company, expected to
> serve and represent the company above all other considerations.
>
> It was at no time formally noted that Catholics, Jews,
> women and Negroes were incapable of response to the indoctri-
> nation, incantations, and Watsonian philosophy prescribed in the
> dictates of IBM. . . . IBM did not create this aspect of the American
> character; rather, it exemplified it and subscribed to it.[12]

As part of this ambience of exclusivity, the benefits that came
with IBM's abundant profits were not extended to the entire community, as Johnson had done with Endicott Johnson's profits. The benevolent capitalism of George F. Johnson embraced all within the
communities of Johnson City and Endicott; the men in the town jail
received a five-dollar gold piece at Christmas; all children received a
free pair of shoes at Christmas and on birthdays, whether or not their
fathers or mothers worked at EJ. His cafeterias, farmer's markets, golf
course, swimming pools, libraries, recreation centers, etc. were open
to anyone who lived in either town. To the contrary, Watson drew a
visible line around his employees and their families, marking it with
benefits and salaries. The country clubs, the trips, the bonuses, and
benefits went directly to his employees. As to the corporation's benefits to the community at large, Watson encouraged and rewarded
noblesse oblige on the part of his employees. IBM men received
bonuses during their annual reviews for their service on community

boards and their charity work. But through their emulation of the charitable behavior of the upper classes, IBM employees increased their own social status within their communities. This striking difference in each man's conception of the social responsibility of a corporation led to the community expression in Johnson City that "EJ did for everyone; IBM does for IBM."

Although both Watson and Johnson opposed Prohibition and government regulation of one's drinking habits, their attitudes about alcohol also reflected their contrasting perspectives of social class and demeanor. Watson absolutely forbade liquor at IBM functions and viewed its use as unseemly and as a flagrant violation of the IBM code of conduct, while Johnson, as mentioned, condoned the working-man's drinking of beer. To Johnson's way of thinking, Prohibition was discrimination against the poor man:

> Our attitude . . . has been that the cellars of the rich have no more right to be full of "booze" than the cellars of the poor full of beer. If there is to be prohibition, let it be real. . . . Giving them [the wealthy] the absolute right to stock up indefinitely and use it at their pleasure, while the poor man cannot even get a pint of beer, is the rottenest legislation—bound to bring the worst possible results and make the most trouble of anything that has occurred in many years.[13]

Both successful capitalists, Johnson and Watson used their power and wealth to create a corporate culture and ethos that mirrored their respective social and personal moral philosophies. Johnson championed the laborer and strove to abolish class lines by promoting the natural aristocracy of the working class as a basis for American wealth and by creating middle-class communities for his workers. Watson established an exclusive cadre of upper-middle-class employees, whose leadership would sell the world its technological future and whose vision would guide the less able.

No Way, EJ

As long as Endicott Johnson's economic umbrella arched over the heads of Johnson City's residents, there was little need for change in the community or in the schools. Until the 1960s, when the demise of EJ seemed imminent, Johnson City had been a functional community, where strong consistencies existed between the social structure of each generation and between the social norms and values of almost all who lived within the community.[14] Since its beginning as a "model community" for shoe operatives in the 1890s, its population had consisted primarily of lower-middle-class factory workers and their families. The median years of school completed for Johnson City residents was less than tenth grade in 1960; the average family income was less than $5,000.[15] For decades a "structural consistency" in occupation and social class was transmitted from one generation of shoe workers to the next.

As a functional community, Johnson City's relationship with its schools was one of reciprocity and stability. The leaders of the school district viewed the primary mission of the schools as the preparation of workers for the Endicott Johnson factories. The economic benevolence of EJ was returned through a fresh, energetic, capable supply of labor. If EJ's factory floors did not appeal to some, business and secretarial courses prepared them for the various small businesses of the community. The children of the professionals in the community were channeled into academic courses and sent on to college. If any changes in the curriculum did occur, they primarily benefited the small number of college-bound students or they incorporated new occupational skills. Like many "less well educated communities," the large majority of residents in Johnson City were "less likely to initiate change . . . [or] put effective pressure on educators to initiate changes on their behalf."[16]

But EJ's economic slide during the 1960s disrupted the social and economic equilibrium of the community and set in motion growing community dissatisfaction with the schools. The visible signs of this slide surfaced in 1960 when the company posted the first loss, amounting to $1.5 million, in the history of its operation. In spite of a heroic stock-purchasing effort by the community in 1961 that thwarted an outside takeover of the corporation, the financial bleeding continued until 1969, when the company was sold to a London-based conglomerate.[17] After the Korean War, Endicott Johnson had employed seventeen thousand workers in the county surrounding Johnson City; by 1967 that number had dwindled to six thousand employees, four thousand of whom lived in Johnson City.[18]

In spite of this drastic reduction in the workforce, Endicott Johnson still experienced a labor shortage in the 1960s. Management had difficulty finding replacements for the waves of workers retiring from the factories— five hundred workers each year. In the decade between 1950 and 1960, the number of people in the town sixty-five

years and older increased four times. Not only were the residents getting older, but younger people were migrating from the town in every
age group except females fifteen to twenty-four years and females
over sixty-five.[19] For the first time in its history, Johnson City's population began to decrease in 1960. Younger people who wanted to stay
in the area avoided EJ and sought employment at IBM or other high-
technology industries. They also preferred to live in the newly built
houses of the suburban developments west of the industrial town
rather than in the aging, EJ-built houses in town.

As the family-owned firm struggled to stay afloat, it found itself
unable to pay the real-estate taxes due on its factories in Johnson City
and to subsidize the many community services it had provided
through the years. The firm that had built many of the schools in
town, had provided the cafeterias for school lunches, and had donated
athletic and recreational facilities found itself appealing to the Johnson
City school board for tax forgiveness on its extensive real-estate hold-
ings. The school board, however, had few other sources of revenue
available, as the number of retirees on fixed incomes increased in the
community and complained vigorously when their taxes were hiked.
The board questioned how it could maintain current student programs, let alone repair or replace its aging buildings.

The Schools Begin to Break Away from EJ

Increasingly weighted down by the gloomy reality of an industry
singing its swan song, the school board was also being pressured from
the New York State Department of Education to centralize its schools
through consolidation with the nine small, surrounding districts as a
means of increasing efficiency and improving student programs.

Centralization through the consolidation of smaller school districts into one larger district has altered historically not only the physical but the political, economical, and curricular structure of American
schooling. Beginning with the common school movement and recurring throughout the history of American education, centralization
occurred most rapidly during the Progressive Era and the age of the
scientific management of schools. To reduce political partisanship, to
increase educational efficiency, and to increase the power of educational experts, schools throughout the country were unified under the
leadership of a new breed of school administrators, "managers of
virtue," who were trained in the latest principles of scientific manage-

ment and in the latest educational innovations.[20] In the eight years between 1917 and 1925, tens of thousands of the smaller units of schools were eliminated. The push for the centralization of schools reemerged in the 1950s to reduce the power of the local community. In 1932, there were 127,531 local basic administrative units in the United States; by 1953, this number had been reduced by over 50 percent to 55,000.

To nudge recalcitrant districts to centralize, state educational departments drafted reports in the 1950s touting the educational benefits students would receive. The reports argued that larger "comprehensive" high schools offered students a more extensive offering of programs at much lower costs than the average school districts could provide.[21] Such reports underscored the inefficiency of the operation of smaller districts but did not mention that, politically, these centralized districts would also reduce local control of the schools through school boards elected at large rather than by geographic area. Cognizant of smaller districts' resistance to being gobbled up by larger schools, the states dangled considerably sized carrots of "increased aid" before them. States offered to pay large shares of the cost of building new elementary and secondary schools by providing long-term, low-interest bonds to finance the district's share of the capital indebtedness.

Between the two world wars, the Village of Johnson City had participated in similar centralization efforts. Like many other towns, it had annexed surrounding areas and accommodated these additional pupils through new buildings. Then, in 1956, the New York State Education Department conducted a "thorough" study of the Johnson City School District, including all schools within the village limits and the nine surrounding districts, to determine the advisability of the centralization of the districts. Not surprisingly, the study recommended that "a merger of [the] districts was extremely desirable and would result in a better educational program for all at a cost that would be equalized across the entire district."[22]

For two years, the board took no action on the study, as the centralization issue smoldered in the community. In 1959, the board publicly introduced the proposal but withdrew it quickly after a vocal group of citizens in one of the outlying districts actively opposed the initiative. Sharing the tax load of the total district meant a definite rise in taxes for this group, while other citizens in the nine outer districts wanted to retain their right to choose whether their children attended the Johnson City High School or a high school in another district.

In the wake of the first outside bid to take over Endicott Johnson, the school board recognized its need to become less dependent upon the tax revenues from Endicott Johnson and held a public referendum on the issue in 1962, a referendum that voters soundly defeated. The debate raged for another two years amid growing signs of EJ's financial distress. In 1964 the centralization referendum was passed and the Central School District No. 2, Towns of Union, Maine, Chenango, and Dickinson (Johnson City is a political subdivision in the town of Union) was democratically established.[23] "Jubilant" board members told the press, "The overwhelming vote supports our confidence in the people of this community. When the chips are down, they do the right thing. They have always done this . . . Johnson City is not really a dying town."[24]

Through centralization Johnson City and its schools had taken their first step in scrubbing away their identity as a shoe town with "greaser schools" and in establishing their independence from EJ's financial vicissitudes. Pulling itself out of the economic cradle of EJ, the community began to fend for itself. What the existing school board did not anticipate was the political window centralization opened for community residents who had had very little input into the decision-making process of the schools.

The Self Within Community

For decades, life in Johnson City had been good, secure, and stable. Children grew up in a working-class community and developed a sense of personal identity and belonging. An active agent in maintaining the EJ ethos, both economically and socially, the schools had supported this life by preparing their students to fit the occupational needs of corporation and community. As Peshkin noted, in a functional community, "neither by learning nor by aspiration are the community's children sharply distinguished from their parents." Both young and old shared feelings about "where to live and what to believe."[25] This sense of the common good and purpose was not only accepted, but welcomed. These shared feelings of nurturance and community intimacy kept people together within the community and discouraged occupational and residential mobility that might jeopardize the intergenerational stability.

According to Coleman, this stability and its "intergenerational closure" provided resources for parents, especially for the most disadvantaged parents with the least personal resources.

A functional community augments the resources available to parents in their interactions with school, in their supervision of their children's associations, both with others their own age and with adults. The feedback that a parent receives from friends and associates, either unsolicited or in response to questions provides extensive additional resources that aid the parent in monitoring the school and the child, and the norms that parents, as part of their everyday activity, are able to establish act as important aids in socializing children.[26]

The blanket of comfort the EJ ethos wrapped around Johnson City emphasized the importance of community as a whole unit where the self was one together with many others in common purpose. The economic success of Endicott Johnson and its corporate welfarism had provided the comforts of a middle-class life for all in the group without the isolating aspects of individual success.

But in the process of sustaining the structural and value consistencies of Johnson City, covert social and financial limitations and restrictions were placed upon the freedom of the individual to maximize his or her own potential. The family, the school, and the community acted in concert to constrain the individual in terms of personal freedom, mobility, academic achievement, occupational choice, and financial success. The legacy of EJ was clear. As long as the Endicott Johnson Corporation was the dominant economic force in the community, the role of "EJer" was handed from generation to generation. Choices made by the individual and for the individual were limited by consideration of the whole and proscribed when they jeopardized the sustainability of the community. In the EJ "co-operative commonwealth," provisions for the good of all entailed the sacrifice of social, economic, and educational opportunities by many and reserved the highest level of occupational, financial, and social success for a select few.

But the decline of Endicott Johnson, the opportunities of IBM, and the accompanying socioeconomic changes and perceptions threw the intergenerational stability of the once-functional community out of kilter at the same time the structural, political changes of centralization were drastically changing the shape of schooling in Johnson City. The harmonious, reciprocal relationship of school and community became fractious and unpredictable. As the traditional social values of the EJ ethos began to collide with the more cosmopolitan values of the outside world, new forces rose from the ranks of the second and third generations of EJ factory workers to grab the power of the schools and shape a new vision for Johnson City's children.[27] This new generation valued higher education and wanted a middle-class life for themselves and their children. They had found jobs at IBM and other technological firms or worked in middle-class professions. They were no longer satisfied with the Johnson City they had inherited from their parents.

4

A Daring New Vision

The community's vote to centralize
the nine surrounding school districts with the Johnson City district
made front-page news the next day. Mrs. Margaret Pauling, school-
board president and wife of a prominent lawyer in Johnson City,
expressed her pleasure with the results in the article. "I feel this is an
expression of confidence by the people. I feel especially happy about
the substantial margin by which it passed. It should make future plans
easier for the new board."[1]

Socially well connected and an active member of the prestigious
Johnson Memorial Church, Pauling viewed her role as a school trustee
as her personal contribution to the civic health of her community.
Except for her sex, Pauling typified Johnson City school-board
trustees: affluent, primarily male, professionals or business owners of
English or Irish stock. These "town fathers" and an occasional "town
mother" regularly contributed their time and effort to determining the
governance of the schools and of other community political, social,
and religious organizations. Interested in the economic and social
well-being of the community, these citizens guided the common affairs
of the community as they pursued their interpretation of the public
good.[2]

Their contributions to their community were interwoven with
what Tocqueville would have called "self-interest properly understood."[3] The school-policy decisions on curriculum made by Pauling
and the other trustees through the decades had provided a ready supply of workers for Endicott Johnson's factories and the town's businesses, and also ensured that their own children had the benefits of an

academic track that prepared them for college and occupations of their own social class and status. Tocqueville thought such enlightened self-interest did "not inspire great sacrifices, but every day it prompts some small ones; by itself it cannot make a man virtuous, but its discipline shapes a lot of orderly, temperate, moderate, careful, and self-con-trolled citizens."[4] These small sacrifices of time and effort gradually and unconsciously inculcated "habits" of civic virtue that sustained the public good and maintained a community consensus of the mean-ing of their common goals.

Having presided over the school board during those years in which the community had been slapped by the financial misfortunes of Endicott Johnson, Pauling supported centralization as a means of decreasing the school's reliance upon EJ, maintaining existing pro-grams for the academically oriented students, and developing voca-tional facilities for the district's children whose future was no longer guaranteed by the shoe industry. Planning to run for a seat on the new district board created by centralization, Pauling saw little conflict between her own social class's self-interest and the community's pub-lic interest. Her personal identification with the community's interest through years of public service had led her to believe that "to harm the town would be to harm oneself."[5]

However, this process of moral identification in which self-interest and community interest are tightly interwoven is fragile in its dependence upon "homogeneous, well-integrated" communities such as Johnson City and those that Tocqueville described. The weaving of self-interest and common interest relies on what John Dewey termed the "integrated principle" of the community. Dewey stated that "a community as a *whole* involved not merely a variety of associative ties which held persons together in diverse ways, but an organization of all elements by an integrated principle."[6] In this inte-grated principle lay the "source of the public" that supported, fed, and shaped the ethos of a community. Herein lay the individual's perception that there were consequences beyond the person and the associations directly concerned with them. The individual sensed that the social actions of each individual were embedded and inter-related in a wide circle of many interests bound by a commonly held, integrated principle that worked to sustain all at a mutually accept-able level.

Dewey believed that democracy in its "generic sense" was the search for the "great community" in which the interests of the individ-ual were held in balance by those interests and goods that were common.[7] In a democracy each person had a dual capacity as an individual with self-interests and as a member of a group with common interests and good.

In the dual capacity of each public person, whether the person was a voter or an elected official, Dewey claimed "the most serious problem of government" arose. This problem was the challenge of putting the interests of the common good above the private interests of the self and led to conflict between the genuine aims and actions of the public and those possessed in private roles.

> Those concerned in government are still human beings. They retain their share of the ordinary traits of human nature. They still have private interests to serve and interests of special groups, those of the family, clique, or class to which they belong. Rarely can a person sink himself in his political function; the best which most men attain to is the domination by the public weal of their other desires.[8]

In Dewey's utilitarian conception of the public, the "invisible hand" of the public weal would cause good will to "arise out of the spontaneous interplay among local businessmen whose individual self-interest is tempered by concern for social respectability and affection for their community."[9] The power of this invisible hand lay in the integrated principle, the ethos of the community, which bound people together and fused a moral identification with a commonly perceived interest.

In Johnson City in the 1960s, the rope of the EJ ethos that had bound the community in a reciprocating sense of mutual, collective interest was unraveling and revealed the fragile nature of the bond between ethos and cultural context. The crumbling of Endicott Johnson's long-standing economic foundation, the ascent of IBM as the premier corporation in the area, and the rapid changes in the community's demographic and social conditions had cracked the cultural ground of the community. Experiencing their own reformation through centralization, the structure of the schools shook as the community around them also changed swiftly. All of these volatile economic, social, and political forces combined to threaten the community's agreement as to the meaning of the public good that Pauling and other town mothers and fathers had shaped. A new vision of the public good and new answers to the question of "cui bono?" began to emerge.

Insurrection at the Polls

In the three weeks prior to the special school-board election in spring 1964, several challengers tossed their hats into the ring for seats on the new board in addition to those recommended by a nominating committee composed of former board members, town business owners, and professionals. Four of these challengers united with a supportive citizen's group and began a relentless, vociferous, door-to-door campaign throughout the community to unseat former incumbents and the nominated candidates.

This group of aggressive challengers were the college-educated sons of Eastern European EJ workers; they were either self-employed or employed at IBM. Unlike many others of their generation who had left Johnson City, they had stayed to raise their young families. They had decided to run to break the grip of those who had ruled the district for decades.

> Why did we run? Well, we felt that the school district under the existing superintendent was run—this may be too strong a word—too dictatorial[ly]. He used an ancient method of "divide and conquer." He had no cabinet, no meeting of principals. He would seek advice individually, but did things much in his own way. Johnson City was like a lot of districts then. People were on the board more as prestigious positions than as responsible positions. People who were on our board were prominent citizens: lawyers, doctors. The four of us challenging them really did not have that type of background to fall back on or to tout to people as important.[10]

They had a different vision for the school system and wanted a "cohesive district . . . with new ideas and new input."[11] They were determined to provide ways for all of the children in the school district to succeed in school, not just the children of the prominent citizens. "The district needed to become progressive. The school was run the way it always had been."[12]

> We campaigned hard, talked to the media. A lot of boards were secretive, again, a strong word, they did not feel a need to discuss school business in front of people. We were very willing to discuss our ideas with the media which was willing to print them. We were well organized, but not well financed.[13]

The group sensed

> important decisions were going to made. They had to be made by
> people who were sensitive to the community, to what they could
> afford, and to all aspects of the community.[14]

After a hotly contested election that ran through several ballots
and into the wee hours of the following morning, three of the four
challengers defeated incumbents, including Pauling. The next morning's edition of the newspaper blared, "Mrs. Pauling Loses JC Board
Seat" in the "sweep of three seats on the new board by a group of
young insurgents in Johnson City."[15]

The New Board Goes to Work

A few months into public office, the new school board commissioned
Syracuse University to conduct a study of the district's existing secondary curriculum and to make recommendations for its improvement. These recommendations on the program would be used to guide
the construction of a new high school for the district and to sell the
need for a new high school to the public.

The survey continued a tradition begun in the Progressive Era
by the educational establishment to use scientifically gathered information to "mold public opinion in its constructive attitude toward
education."[16] First used to "rate and standardize" schools, the surveys

> showed citizens the complexity of social engineering done by
> superintendents, exposed the need for new funds and buildings,
> instructed boards about how to delegate decisions to the superin-
> tendent, and suggested more effective modes of teaching.[17]

These rational, scientifically designed instruments also recommended
that the decision making of schools be done by the educational experts
and be removed from the whims of local politics and private interests.

Suspicious of the nature of previous decision making, the new
board wished to rely upon the "facts" to uncover and solve problems.
When the two hundred-page survey was presented to the board in
1966, it criticized almost every area of the present curriculum that had
been "proposed for secondary schools forty years ago" and noted the
lack of an "articulated, well intentioned curriculum with systemized

objectives or basic rationale."[18] Referring to the high turnover of teachers in almost every subject area and the resulting inexperience of the staff, it recommended professional staff development to improve curriculum, to better meet the needs of its students, and to improve coordination and communication among teachers within individual curricular areas. Only the interscholastic athletic programs, the music department, and the newly formed pupil personnel program received high ratings.

But the survey report reserved its strongest criticism for the organization of the district-wide administrative staff and stressed that poor communication between administration and staff was a major weakness. Too many decisions were made by the superintendent and the school board without any staff input or knowledge. Staff members interviewed were "unable to identify the formal procedures by which learning experiences and program objectives were brought together meaningfully for the whole school district."[19] Most administrations positions had "'grown like topsy' with little consideration given to their 'fit' into a total organizational pattern and in some cases, with little regard for the suitability of the incumbent."[20] The survey strongly recommended that the superintendent "free himself for broad planning and leadership" and "let go of the reins."

As for the school board, "in too many instances, members of the board were involved with administrative decisions."[21] Forgoing subtle hints, the report boldly acknowledged that the present board was not a consensus board and that "disagreements among board members are healthy and desirable," but found it "imperative that appropriate machinery be established to reconcile these differences so that the school program is not disrupted."[22]

In response to the survey, the superintendent and board initiated immediate curricular changes for a secondary reading program and for a third track, the "Basic Curriculum," for "meeting the needs of a group of teenagers who can not be successful in the academic programs of the junior and senior high school . . . [and] who should be encouraged to remain in school until graduation."[23]

As both the administration and board mulled over the results of the survey, subsequent board elections in 1966 and 1967 produced a majority of IBM-employed citizens on the board, who joined with the "young insurgents" to form a voting bloc. Although these "IBMers" did not hold high positions in the corporation, they represented Johnson City's new middle class and reflected those values Watson had instilled into all levels of his firm. This bloc first tangled with the nascent Johnson City Teachers Association (JCTA) and refused to recognize the group as the duly elected bargaining agent for the district's teachers under the guidelines of the New York Taylor Law on collective bargaining.

In the midst of the cantankerous exchange with the JCTA over the pending teachers' contract in fall 1967, the board decided to fire the district's successful football coach, Frank Dilman. Johnson City, known locally for its rampant enthusiasm for its athletic teams, had a tradition of winning football games and easily drew twelve thousand spectators to each of its games. Responding to the shock of Dilman's dismissal and angry that Dilman had first learned of his dismissal through a telephone call from a local news reporter, the JCTA fired off letters of support from the director of athletics, the building principal, the superintendent, and the association. The community was outraged over the firing and hounded the board to reveal its reason for the dismissal. Refusing to discuss its reasons for the dismissal publicly, the board shielded itself with a state policy that prohibited the public discussion of school personnel matters.

For five months, the controversy raged through the community. In the midst of this tempest, the board in early 1968 abruptly announced that it had voted not to renew the contract of the district superintendent, Robert Muncie. Muncie, a former president of the teachers' association, had risen through the ranks to the position of superintendent over a thirty-three-year period. He had supported the football coach in the aftermath of Dilman's firing and had knocked heads repeatedly with the board on the control of district policy. Choir director at the Johnson Memorial Church and a long-time associate of the community's old guard, Muncie represented all that this board was trying to undo in the community. Again, the board refused to discuss with the public its reason for the termination.

Reacting with "shock and deep regret," the JCTA immediately responded to the public announcement with the association's full support of the superintendent. During the next several months, the school board was besieged with phone calls, personal letters by the PTA and community members, and letters to the editor demanding a public hearing. The board replied that whether to have a public meeting was the board's decision, not the public's. As the community-school conflict raged, the board made only two concessions to the superintendent and the public. First, the board unanimously agreed to offer him employment for two years as a consultant to the district until his retirement was vested.[24] Second, in a public meeting the board stated that the justification for the firing of Muncie could be found in the Syracuse University survey and that copies had been placed in the town and district libraries.

Although the superintendent had the support of almost all of the school personnel as well as a devoted group of community residents, overall the community barely responded to the firing at the annual election of the school board. Voter turnout was the second lowest of the four years; the budget passed easily; and of the two challengers who ran for the one vacant board seat, another IBM employee won. During the next three years, the board and two interim superintendents completed the new high school and in 1971 began the search for a superintendent who could act upon their vision for the children of Johnson City. The ill will generated by the board's dismissal of Muncie and Dilman went underground to fester through the next decade and eventually erupted to threaten the vision of the IBM-controlled board.

The Changing Meaning of the Public Good

Freed from the social and economic constraints of the world of Endicott Johnson in which their parents had labored, the new centralized school board wanted to update schooling "forty years old" and raise the academic levels and aspirations for all children in the Johnson City district. The board's interpretation of the public good grew out of their own common experiences, but was also typical of the "new middle class" in the 1960s. In their study of a functional community, *Small Town in Mass Society*, Vidich and Bensman analyzed the importance of school issues in the lives of the middle class during this period. They stated,

> The new middle class lives with the school issue through the lives
> of its children. This is a process that commands their attention on
> a daily and weekly basis. . . . When presented with an issue . . . of
> education . . . that affects its children, the middle class responds
> not in terms of higher moral values but in terms of self-interest.[25]

Deciding to live in Johnson City instead of moving out to the suburbs, the new board wanted to change the schools to benefit their own children and to serve their own interests. But in doing so, they set in motion a series of educational changes that would raise the educational levels of all children and, ultimately, increase the prosperity of the whole community. Although there were those who disagreed with the board's actions, the majority of voters in Johnson City voted to elect and reelect these board members and thereby signified their agreement with the board's actions and policies. In this sense, the board's enlightened self-interest represented the shaping of a new integrated principle for Johnson City, one rooted in technology, self-sufficiency, middle-class values, and the IBM ethos.

However, their response to some constituents' demands for a public explanation of the firing of the coach and superintendent was both problematic and paradoxical when viewed from Dewey's conception of a social democracy. By refusing to answer their public's questions, the board utilized their representative power to squelch the political discourse of segments of their community and to limit the social action of democracy. Their actions to free the district from the autocratic rule of Superintendent Muncie mimicked the very behavior they had despised and undermined their preelection promises of public input into school decision making. To justify their actions, they took refuge in the research and recommendations of the survey conducted by the educational experts.

Public justification of their actions revealed their own interpretation of the public good and signaled the beginning of a new principle for the district and community. In the first fifty years of Johnson City's existence, George F. Johnson had constructed a meaning of the public good through his own precepts of a cooperative commonwealth and the moral pursuit of individual virtue; during the next two decades Pauling and other town leaders had formed a meaning of the public good based upon their own enlightened self-interest and the maintenance of existing social and economic relationships in the functional community. The new board constructed its own meaning of the public good from the enlightened self-interest of a new middle class and upon the technical advice of experts.

In *Habits of the Heart*, Bellah et al. explored the meaning of the public good for "civic-minded professionals" like the young, college-educated IBM technicians and managers on the new Johnson City school board.[26] A "utilitarian individualism" that "asserts that individuals can know their long-term interests in today's complex world only by careful research into the consequences of different courses of action" shapes this meaning.[27] The civic-minded professional believes that careful consideration of this research by political leaders who are "well-educated, bright, and dedicated" will yield neutral, technical solutions that will serve the interests of a community in the most just manner.

This faith in the neutrality and fairness of expert, scientifically researched solutions led the Johnson City school board to commission the 1966 survey on the secondary school curriculum. They believed that the report's research and recommendations would free their decisions from the class biases hidden in the policies of Pauling, the old-guard school trustees, and Superintendent Muncie.

However, Bellah et al. warned that balancing of self-interest and public interest through neutral, technical solutions was precariously perched upon two hidden assumptions. First, such a conception of the public good rested upon the belief that the interests of all groups in the community are not "fundamentally incompatible—so that one contending group does not permanently have to sacrifice its welfare for the good of another or for the good of society as a whole." This required the belief that a solution existed whereby all parties could benefit. In a steadily expanding economy such as Johnson City had under Endicott Johnson, where everyone's standard of living was steadily increased through the EJ subsidies, such a harmony of interests occurred. Although IBM did not directly extend its economic largess to every citizen throughout the community, it provided economic opportunity for the area's residents and added substantial wealth to the overall expanding economy of the region. But in a zero-sum economy without either corporate paternalistic care for a community or a rapidly expanding economy, "one group becomes richer only at the cost of making others poorer." When the supply of benefits is limited, benefits received by one group entail the sacrifice of another and can lead to conflict over which group should receive the greater benefit.[28] Firmly grounded in the technological lore of IBM and raised in the EJ ethos by their parents, the behavior of the Johnson City school boards of the late 1960s and 1970s revealed this first assumption. They believed that they had been elected by the community to develop a school system where all could succeed, go to college, and, possibly, get a job at IBM. If anything had to go, it was the entrenched values of the established elite of the community and the attitudes that the occupation of a child's parents determined his or her curriculum. By seeking and supporting an educational philosophy that promised ever-expanding educational benefits for all children in the community, the new board believed they were acting in the best interests of the community.

A second hidden assumption was the belief that "technical expertise and the ability to carry out research" qualified one to be a leader. This required the belief that the solutions of experts were grounded in highly reliable, impartial data. This belief ignored ongoing debates regarding the accuracy and validity of social-science data based upon the behavior and motives of human beings. It also denied the possibility that a rational leader's action could be tainted by personal ambition or greed.

Rule by managers and scientists in a democratic society also posed the inherent danger of "administrative despotism," which gently bent the will of citizens through restraining, enervating governmental regulations and procedures. Tocqueville feared this form of rule more than the enlightened self-interest of the town leaders, for he claimed, "Under this system the citizens quit their state of dependence just long enough to choose their masters and then fall back into it."[29] By placing their faith in a public good shaped by civic-minded, middle-class professionals, would the schools of Johnson City exchange the rule of the autocratic Muncie for a new despot whose power lay in expert, rational planning?

5

The Rigorous Wrestlers of Power

Two Platonic questions—"Who rules?" and "With what justification?"—frame the second major problem in understanding the development of outcome-based education in Johnson City and its meaning for educational reform. Much has been written on the importance of instructional and transformational leadership in the reform of schools, but the primary emphasis has been upon the characteristics and behavior of the leader. Little attention has been given to the reciprocal interaction of the leaders with those who join with the leader to change schools—the "led." The following chapters explore the complexity of this relationship and the ethical dimensions of establishing a consensus for change in the process of successful educational reform.

The question "Who rules a school district?" usually elicits a response naming the official leader of the district, the person who is legally appointed by the locally elected school board after a quasi-public review process, i.e., the superintendent. But whether or not this person holds both the formal and the informal power to rule the district resides in the more difficult second question, "With what justification?"

Justification, defined as "the act of demonstrating or proving oneself to be just, right, or valid," involves purposeful human action that is rational or ethical or both.[1] Valid rule of a school district lies in the legal appointment by the school board and is generally determined by a superintendent's demonstration of expertise and credentials. The justness or rightness of the superintendent's actions, however, is connected and entwined with the other human beings in schools, those who carry out these decisions and who are directly or indirectly affected by them. Underlying each of these human interactions is the cultural context of schooling where human interests agree or conflict and where the outer community's purposes for schooling compete for its resources.

Within this complexity of interests and purposes, a leader constructs meaning of the school's context and thinks through his or her own value positions within this meaning before acting. In this process, the leader has "two bounden duties": (1) to know through rational analysis where the school as an educational organization stands; and (2) to be committed to that stand through a moral analysis of his or her own personal values and the values of the organization.[2] To justify actions to himself or herself and to others in schooling, a leader must not only know what can be done and how it can be done, but whether it should be done.

But knowledge and moral commitment do not complete the justification of a leader's actions. Justification is lame if the leader's actions do not connect with the expectations and actions of those being led. How can rulers justify their leadership if no one is willing to follow their actions or directives?

A leader's movement from ideas and values to action involves mediation by the other people in the group or organization. The nature of the axis lying between the leader and the led determines their continued interaction and is a common field for both. Herein lies a dialectic of power. A leader may possess the legal and moral power of the school district and may have a whole range of techniques of coercion or persuasion, learned over the long history of leadership or administration, to induce others to follow the leader's actions. But the leader can be rendered impotent if the others refuse to follow. A superintendent can have all the official power, but if the teachers, the central administration, principals, staff, the students, the parents, the community, and so forth use their influence or diffused power to resist, he or she cannot lead. Dialectically, it is the follower who determines the real power of the leader. "The follower not only has power. He/she has ultimate power."[3]

The "rigorous wrestling" of ideas and values between the leader and those who are led, as Cremin noted, lies at the heart of education reform. When this heart of the process is somehow left in less capable hands, reform movements become "procedure and little else."[4] By analyzing and understanding this dialectic of power, we explore the heart of Johnson City's ODDM and begin to comprehend why OBE and other educational reforms are so seldom duplicated in other school districts.

Initiating Change

In fall 1971, the newly hired superintendent, Jack Champlin, entered a school district and community in economic, social, and political transition. The industrial paradigm and work ethos symbolized by the once-prominent corporation of Endicott Johnson was giving way to the technological, professional ethos of IBM and the smaller technological firms in the area. The beliefs, values, and way of living of a majority of the community's residents, grown old working in the shoe factories, were gradually being displaced by those of a small group of upwardly mobile, middle-class residents with young families represented by the IBM-employee-dominated school board. Their worldview began to form a new ethos for the district and the community. Their quest for the rational expansion of educational opportunities for their children overrode the emotional appeals of the old-timers who argued for retaining the vestiges of the old Johnson City and the EJ ethos.

A self-declared agent of change, Champlin impressed the board and the teachers with the instructional program he had implemented in his former district. During his interview, he forthrightly described his vision for the four thousand students in the Johnson City schools; it was based upon the premises of what he called the "open structured school," a program "deeply rooted in learning theory—especially the idea that most children can achieve mastery of subject matter when proper provision is made for individual learning rates and styles."[5] Champlin dazzled the technologically oriented board with his references to research and his instructional knowledge, based upon indices and learning rates.

Recalling his entrance into the district, Champlin stated

> I had a clear message and I was not going to compromise. The school board could tell me what they wanted and I would tell them "how." If they didn't like it, then they could fire me. I re-educated the board to the belief that all children can learn. And with that knowledge they had to support the program.[6]

As soon as he was hired, Champlin began the implementation of this program in Johnson City's smallest elementary school, Oakdale, where a group of eight elementary teachers had already begun experimenting with individualized learning in their classrooms. Working directly under his supervision, these teachers began to incorporate a system of individualized learning in an open-classroom plan. The students worked individually on tasks to mastery with teacher guidance or were flexibly grouped for instruction according to achievement level and not chronological age. By October 1971, Champlin handed the board the outline of his program encompassing the mastery approach to learning to be implemented in kindergarten through twelfth grade in the coming years.

His second action was the formation of what he termed a "redesign task force" comprised of one hundred members, including administration, professional staff, students, and citizens.[7] Once established by the board, the task force attended a series of programs by outside experts on the most recent "advances in learning theory and behavioral research . . . on the changes in structures of schools . . . and alternatives in organizing schools and learning environments." After this orientation—or, as one resident called it, "brainwashing"—the task force prepared several recommendations for the board on the implementation of the open-structured learning environment throughout the district and the reorganization of the district facilities; it even proposed recommendations for the revitalization of the ailing community.[8]

Early in the school year, Champlin also received board approval to institute a summer in-service for teachers in grades K–8 whereby the teachers involved would become the "change agents and trainers in their own building, therefore, providing a multiplier effect in developing skills of fellow staff members."[9] Champlin's belief in training the district's own teachers as instructional leaders who would instruct, assist, and mentor their peers on the curricular programs and strategies of his vision would become a critical factor in the achievement of the program's positive academic gains. He regularly met with these teachers and worked to develop a professional relationship with them. His confidence in their efficacy to implement his vision served as a psychological reward for their efforts. At the same time, he aggressively pressured those teachers resisting change "to get with the program or get out of the way."[10] The building principals served as first lieutenants to provide the daily supervision of the teachers' program and were often reassigned or fired when their commitment to Champlin's vision wavered.

Without a doubt, Champlin hit the ground running in Johnson City. In six months he clearly articulated an instructional belief system for the district and began the implementation of the "theoretical" as defined by Sarason. Intuitively understanding his school board's faith in rational planning and their acquiescence in the presence of a data-driven, strong executive officer, Champlin gained and held their support for his plans through a process he called "renorming."[11] This involved regular goal-setting sessions for the board in which Champlin articulated and reviewed the instructional mission of the district and then urged the board to adopt policies stating this mission.

Although his honeymoon as superintendent was filled with aggressive, purposeful actions and little resistance from the other people in the school and community, the full justification of his leadership was not to be so easy. "If leadership should seem to be easy, then beware. In all probability something is, or is about to be, going wrong."[12]

Coming of age as an educator in established middle-class communities, Champlin was not prepared for the swirling complexity of the diverging, competing interests and values extant in the social culture of Johnson City in the aftermath of EJ's collapse. Champlin arrived at the cusp of a new era for a community where the stuff of its culture, the substance of its values, interests, and actions, the so-called social-institutional context of the school, was in a state of change and turmoil.

Conflict

Tremors within the turbulent cultural ground of the district began to be felt in February 1972, when community and staff resistance to the new program coalesced sufficiently to defeat soundly the budget referendum for the building of a new middle school designed to showcase Champlin's instructional program. The next sign of discord occurred when the president of the Johnson City Teachers' Association (JCTA) publicly requested that the board reject Champlin's recommendation to eliminate eight curriculum director positions and to hire his former colleague Al Mamary as assistant superintendent. Ignoring the JCTA's request, the board approved Champlin's proposal. By the end of his first year, community discontent reached a flash point when a group of residents confronted the board with a petition demanding that "the new program . . . in Oakdale . . . be submitted to the voters in a referendum." Denouncing the petition as "a Salem witch hunt," Champlin praised those teachers "who had the guts and integrity" to implement the program.[13]

Upon the advice of its solicitor, the board determined that it was the "prerogative and responsibility of the professional staff to determine the educational program of the district" and not the community's.[14] Nonetheless, the animosity toward Champlin and the new program continued as teachers opposed to the program aligned with EJ retirees and ethnic groups in the community to fight Champlin.

Older residents, already feeling the strain of increased taxes as a result of Johnson City's eroding industrial tax base and the deteriorating economy of New York State, feared the additional tax increases from the new programs and buildings. The elderly united with the voters of Eastern European descent, whose ethnic pride Champlin had insulted with careless comments during his first year in the community. Several sources agreed that

> In a short time he managed to rub a lot of the people the wronway. . . . Said he wouldn't live in Johnson City because there wasn't a house there fit to live in. Once, in a public meeting, he called the community a bunch of peasants, of peons who didn't know which way to go. Said he was a Scotch man in a beer community.[15]

In spite of the simmering dissent, implementation of mastery learning continued. No longer using the unpopular word "open" to describe the program, Champlin personally helped teachers in two other elementary schools to implement the "personalized learning program for individuals based upon mastery." As Champlin continued to "renorm" the school board, the board consistently endorsed his initiatives and in June 1973 formally adopted Champlin's "Learning Environment Goal" for the entire district.[16]

By the end of his second year, however, the community launched a major attack on both Champlin and his program. After crushing the annual budget for the upcoming school year in the June referendum, the first budget defeat in the district's history, residents stormed the board meeting with a petition signed by one thousand of the seven thousand eligible voters in the district. The document stated, "We the undersigned are disgusted with the performance of Dr. J. R. Champlin and urge the school board to remove him from the district."[17]

Again the board refused to recognize the community's right to control either the curriculum or personnel. Nonetheless, the community continued to display its power to curtail Champlin's initiatives by defeating annual budgets and throwing school-board incumbents out of office repeatedly. In the eleven years Champlin served as superintendent of the district, the community defeated five annual budgets, forcing the district to operate on austerity budgets. In the same period, five incumbent school-board members were ousted by newcomers who ran on a platform to "get Champlin out of the school district."[18] Upset by an unpopular superintendent and an unresponsive school board, Johnson City residents sought out every avenue available to them—petitions, the press, community meetings, and the voting booth—to unseat those who, in their eyes, misused the public power they had entrusted to them. Providing a classic example of the dissatisfaction theory of school governance as described by Iannacone and Lutz, the Johnson City community wanted to boot Champlin out of the district.[19]

The ongoing wrestling for power between Champlin and the traditional forces of the community was most clearly dramatized during two periods of contract disputes with the teachers' association, the last of which would lead to his retirement.

In spring 1976, New York's economic conditions became worse in the wake of the national oil shortage and with the impending bankruptcy of New York City. Severely disadvantaged by the state's education funding formula, the district was being penalized for the large assessed value of the empty EJ factories, contributing almost no tax revenue. With the board's consent, Champlin made an effort to hold the line on school taxes for the upcoming, financially lean year by approaching the JCTA's president with a proposal that did not increase local taxes. In exchange for a one-year salary freeze from the teachers, the board would rescind its proposal to cut eighteen teachers in the upcoming budget. Champlin had already pruned several teaching positions in the past five years through retirement and resignation after "both careful and continuing assessment," actions seen by many teachers as his means of eliminating those who did not agree with his new program.[20]

However, the JCTA president, Frank Dilman, was none other than the football coach who had been fired by the board several years before. After the JCTA unanimously rejected the board's offer, its president countered with its own cost-cutting proposal reducing Champlin to a supervising principal and eliminating several administrative positions. In the next six months a war of words ripped through the school and community as the board and Champlin fought with the JCTA and its allies in the community over the teaching positions and the budget. Even the high school students entered the fray by staging a walkout in support of the teachers. Crowds met, defeated the annual budget, filed petitions, and railed against Champlin in letters to the local newspaper editor.

Creating a political turmoil in the community that neither Champlin nor the board had anticipated, the staff reduction issue inflamed many residents outside the hard core of those who had opposed Champlin ever since he was hired. In spite of several efforts by Champlin to mend fences with the community in the four previous years, the community's bitterness over grievances from the firings of the coach and superintendent, fear over the uncertain economic and social conditions, and wounded pride bound the community together in their fight for the teachers' jobs.

Vowing to stop Champlin and the board, the JCTA called for a teachers' strike, the first strike in the history of Johnson City, for the first day of the new 1976–77 school year. After six months of bitter acrimony in the early morning hours before the opening of school doors, Champlin was able to forge a compromise with the JCTA, saving face for the board, the association, and the community.

Champlin recalled that the district was "back to normal within two weeks after the brutal shootout with the teachers' union" and that the progress of the instructional changes churned on to encompass the high school and to expand into all programs, including the discipline policy for the district.[21] Apparently, the community did not share Champlin's optimism, for community resentment continued and flared at the election booth. Annual budgets were defeated; incumbents were not reelected.

Then a new form of opposition took shape in the election of two board members who had run on an anti-Champlin platform. The second generation sons of Eastern European EJ workers, these two men were well-educated, articulate, and confident leaders. One worked for IBM; the other had just recently quit. In an interview, he stated he was unable to tolerate the constraints IBM employment had placed upon his personality. He also jokingly stated that he "wanted to wear a blue shirt."[22] Together, they worked on the existing board to change their views about Champlin and drew upon support in the community to counter the forceful personality of Champlin. Repeatedly, they challenged his grip on the issues and fought for the control of the board. Yearly, they voted against the rollover of his employment contract.

Their pressure on Champlin continued until 1980, when they finally pulled the rest of the board to their side during a contract dispute with the JCTA. Once again, Champlin had locked horns with Dilman, JCTA's president and former coach, over negotiations. The hatred between the two men flashed as the teachers threatened a work slowdown. After a month of heated exchanges during school board meetings, the board had enough. Under the leadership of the quick-thinking former IBM employee, the board took charge of the situation and directed Champlin to work together to come to an early settlement.[23]

Publicly chastened by this directive and bitten by yet another budget defeat, Champlin began a personal campaign to promote the instructional successes of the district at local and national conferences and in national publications.[24] He also created a chronology of district reports that documented the implementation of mastery learning within the district from 1971 through 1982. At this time, Champlin began his work with others to develop the Network of Outcome-Based Schools, which helped to increase his own visibility outside of the district.[25]

In 1982, after having received the American Association of Superintendents "Leadership for Learning" Award, Champlin announced to the community his retirement from the district to direct the Network of Outcome-Based Schools and to teach as a member of the faculty of a Texas university. With his resignation, the board immediately appointed Albert Mamary as superintendent with the unanimous endorsement of the school board, teachers' association, and community.

The Heart of Reform

In spite of a decade of continuous conflict with the community, Champlin had managed to turn the "greaser" district of the dying, blue-collar shoe factory town into a district nationally recognized for academic excellence. As the next chapter demonstrates, Champlin did not accomplish this alone; he did, however, continuously have to justify his leadership in the face of repeated challenges. He worked persistently to develop and maintain a consensus among people inside and outside of the schools who believed in his vision and committed themselves to the implementation of the program.

Purposeful human conduct in response to the complex, conflicting, contradictory values of the cultural ground surrounding humans
in schooling, the roads taken and not taken, and the decisions made
by both the leader and the led are inevitably embroidered into the
moral fabric of the culture. In Champlin's conflicts with the resistant
forces and values of the school and community, we see starkly the
actions of those who lead and are led and have a sense of "secular
epiphany": glimpses of a past reality in "sudden intuitive flashes" of
the deliberative, conscious act of choosing one action over another.
Here the moral action of educational leadership is most obvious.

Hodgkinson has written that in our understanding of schools we
have neglected a third form of "knowing" that best explains the moral
art of leadership. Vexed by the Marxist appropriation of the term *praxis*
and Marxist limitation of its meaning to "action with political reflection," Hodgkinson in his value theory of educational leadership
reclaimed the term and returned praxis to its Aristotelian meaning of
"ethical action in a political context."[26]

Aristotle reasoned that humans have "three distinctive ways of
knowing; three approaches to the world, three modes of action." They
are *theoria, techne,* and *praxis. Theoria* or theory represents our way of
knowing as we seek to explain the abundant world of sense data constantly bombarding us. Here, the human intellect seeks to account for,
then abstracts, generalizes, induces, or deduces an understanding that
is codified into knowledge and principles through language. *Techne* is
the human mode of knowing applied to matter and material to produce our application or interpretation of our sense data through art,
craft, and technology. Through *techne,* we structure and alter the physical means by which we live. As Hodgkinson asserts, we are most
familiar with these ways of knowing and have even oversubscribed to
a forced dichotomy between theory and practice, between theorist and
practitioner, between researcher and developer. "Such divisions can
lead to worse than mere failure of communication . . . they stem from
a failure of conception," because we lack the meaning of Aristotle's
third term, *praxis.*[27]

Hodgkinson begins simply by stating that praxis is ethical conduct in a political context, but goes on to explain that praxis is a "complex, subtle, but essential concept which suggests a duality in
action."[28] During praxis, in those moments prior to the initiation of an
action within the political complexities of the surrounding context, a
person contemplates conflicting knowledge. In praxis lie "two or more
moments of consciousness or reflection, on one hand, and behavior

and commitment on the other."[29] At the phenomenological level, a human choice is being made, whereby "purposeful human conduct is informed and guided by purposes, intentions, motives, morals, emotions, and values *as well as* the facts or 'science' of the case."[30] In these moments of knowing just prior to action, *theoria* and *techne* are united, and a moral transformation takes place. A decision is framed with ethical implications.

Praxis as ethical conduct in a political context occurs constantly in the human enterprise of schooling and in the ongoing dialectic of power relations that imbue schools and their cultural ground. Praxis circumscribes the conscious act of choosing one action over another, the moral fusion of knowledge and application during an act of leadership. It is a concept that demands both intellectual and intuitive acknowledgment, for it is only partly contained in sense data or matter, and metaphorically speaking, it has a spirit that tends to fly away when the dead text of schooling and the actions therein are examined. It lies in the domain of consciousness and in *values*, a complex, contemplative course in any age and a politically treacherous one in late-twentieth-century schooling in America. Ironically, in this age as we have become more cognizant of the limitations of science, rationality, and theory and have viewed the dark sides of our technological accomplishments, we have become more fearful of the values in our decisions in schools.

An example of American's current fear of the explicit statement of values can be found in the dissemination of outcome-based education. The inclusion of student value outcomes in the school curriculum has fueled a brutal attack upon the OBE reform movement by the fundamentalist right in Pennsylvania, Missouri, Virginia, Connecticut, and other states.[31] This coalition of parents has not fought the process of ethical decision making or praxis but the explicit statement of student outcomes on cultural values in state curriculum mandates. Such political outrage merely underscores the sensitive nature of the role of values in the process of schooling.

The difficulty of describing the praxis of school reform efforts, of fully accounting for the moments of contemplation and reflection that preceded ethical actions in complex, often paradoxical contexts, has also hindered the efforts to replicate examples of externally validated programs of academic success such as ODDM for students. Without an understanding of the ethical dimension of decision making within the political context of the improvement process, the introduction of theory and the application of technology into the complexity of the many purposes of human schooling are simplistic and shallow. As a result, the many feverish attempts to package, transport, and deliver models of OBE and educational reform through a blitzkrieg of conferences and in-service workshops at the national, state, and local levels ring like tin bells. This intense campaign to improve American schools has enriched some, occupied many, and changed little for the bulk of our students and for the way we do schooling in the United States. The startling admission in a 1994 issue of *Outcomes* that "Johnson City continues to shine as the prime example of the power and practicality of OBE"—by the leaders of the Network of Outcome-Based Schools ten years after the group was formed—indicates that something is missing in the replication of models of effective educational change.

6

Praxis and Knowledge/Power

O chestnut-tree, great rooted blossomer,
Are you the leaf, the blossom, or the bole?
O body swayed to music, o brightening glance
How can we know the dancer from the dance?
—W. B. Yeats, "Among School Children"

Outcome-based education has experienced a turbulent ride on the educational reform waves slapping at American schools during the 1980s and 1990s. "Recent disputes over plans to launch outcome-based education (OBE) have left reformers baffled, discouraged, and defensive," declared an article in a leading educational journal in 1994.[1] The author Ron Brandt queried, "Is outcome-based education dead?" as he reviewed the controversies OBE had created in school districts and states where educators pushed its adoption. Yet, in the same article, Brandt recognized the "flourishing" OBE program in Johnson City as one that had "compiled an impressive record of student achievement."

Johnson City's model of OBE had gained national attention during the first wave of educational reform of the 1980s. This wave, termed the excellence movement, focused upon the improvement of school success as measured by student test scores and advocated reforms that stressed assessment, accountability, and the tightening of standards, particularly at the state level.[2]

In the late 1980s, a second wave of reform reports roared for the "restructuring" of schools along the lines of corporate America's reorganization for the postmodern age. In their search for the roots of the

69

economic miracle of postwar Japan, American business had found the principles of the American management theorist and statistician, W. Edwards Deming. Briefly stated, Deming's principles of "total quality management" were based in the belief that the improvement of product and service quality is unlimited when management and employees engage in continuous training, work in cooperative teams, communicate freely, and establish mutual trust. These cooperative teams of management and employees, "quality circles," "empower employees by cultivating and respecting their individual and collective expertise."[3]

In an effort to transcend the limitations of schools' bureaucratic, hierarchical structures with their top-down flow of power, educational policymakers challenged local school organizations by promoting reforms that shifted power from the local bureaucracy of the school district and its administrators to teachers and parents.[4]

The age of efficiency in American schools had built the hierarchical model of schooling in which administrative experts scientifically managed and dictated "education methods and subject-matter to a body of passive, recipient teachers."[5] But by 1984, the educator and reformer Theodore Sizer claimed that the powerless, "compromised" state of America's teachers was a major cause of the poor performance of students:

> Teachers are rarely consulted, much less given significant authority, over the rules and regulations governing the life of their school; these usually come from "downtown." . . . Teaching often lacks a sense of ownership, a sense among teachers working together that the school is theirs. [6]

Report after report underscored Sizer's conclusions and called for the restructuring of schools to increase the power of teachers. Change strategies of the second wave demanded that the "management structure of schools allow teachers more discretion over curricular, instructional, and resource allocation decisions . . . and control over their working conditions."[7]

The "empowerment" of teachers became a buzzword in the educational literature of the late 1980s and 1990s. Seth Kreisberg noted that

> the term *empowerment* has begun to saturate the rhetoric of school reform across the political spectrum. . . . The term has become a mainstay of the Association for Supervision and Curriculum

Development, of teachers' unions, of the school reform movement, and of the teacher education reform movement.[8]

In his book on the nature of power in relationships, Kreisberg established this meaning of empowerment:

> Empowerment comes through mutual dialogue and shared work to improve the lives of particular individuals while at the same time trying to improve the lives of all individuals in a particular community.[9]

As Kreisberg and others noticed, however, the second wave's push for empowerment was directed mainly to teachers through various forms of site-based management; to a lesser extent, it was directed to parents through change strategies advocating types of school choice, parent councils, and home schooling. Rarely was it directed to the students in schools. Referencing Charlotte Perkins Gilman's novel, *The Yellow Wall-Paper*, Kreisberg stated

> For many students, *their* yellow wallpaper is pastel paint on cinder block walls. They are trapped figures—lacking voices that are listened to and respected, and lacking control over their lives.[10]

During this period in which the educational literature espoused the empowerment of teachers through the professionalization of their roles and the expansion of their responsibilities, it also fell unnaturally silent about the power of administrators and the bureaucracies of schooling. The literature avoided the use of the word "power" when discussing principals and superintendents, preferring words such as "moral authority," "commitment," "bonding," mutual exchanges," and "value-added" to describe the leadership of administrators in schools where successful reform practices were occurring.[11]

For example, the 1990 yearbook of the National Society for the Study of Education on educational leadership and administration concentrated on the leadership of schools within the context of communities, families, and schools but did not address in any form the use of power that facilitates such leadership.[12] According to the yearbook, the effective leader in a restructured school in the 1990s

> establishes organizational conditions, such as creating and enabling cohesive work groups that substitute for direct, more autocratic leadership. . . . The principal supports experimentation

and risk through symbolic acts. . . . These acts serve to establish a
collaborative and professional atmosphere, keeping the school
moving forward. These acts legitimize teachers' actions; they say,
"your work is important and accepted, you belong."[13]

No mention was made of *how* the leader establishes these conditions,
enables work groups, or legitimizes teachers' actions. With the spot-
light on teachers' power during this second wave, reference to administrators' power and the means of sharing their power was rare.

Those who led the dissemination of OBE were quick to respond
to this new movement for the empowerment of teachers. Johnson City
educators, including former superintendent Champlin as director of
the National Center for Outcome-Based Education, retained the
model's emphasis upon student performances on cognitive and affective outcomes in schools. However, they asserted that restructuring
schools by empowering teachers was firmly entrenched in the schools
implementing OBE such as Johnson City.

In a 1993 retrospective on the development of outcome-based
education in Johnson City, Champlin viewed OBE as a "total systems
model empowering the user to attain clear, crisp outcome/exit learner
behaviors." Employing J. McGregor Burns's concept of the "transformational leader," one who "influences associates to connect to significance and acts to achieve it," Champlin contended that in OBE,

> the nature of leadership must change from directing and control-
> ling to challenging and empowering. . . . all persons can become
> leaders. Burns makes this very point: sometimes leaders become
> associates and associates become leaders. Imagine the power of a
> school/school district where everyone is a "leader."[14]

In a recent book, *Total Quality Management,* Schmoker and Wilson con-
cur with Champlin's view of leadership in an OBE school and portray
the Johnson City schools as one of the foremost districts in the country demonstrating Edward Deming's management principles.[15]

William Glasser, a psychiatrist who has written extensively on
student failure and success in public schools, has also identified the
Johnson City Schools as "the best quality school model around."[16]
For Glasser, a "quality school" implemented his own control theory
and utilized the proven quality methods of W. Edwards Deming.[17]
In quality schools, the traditional form of management, "boss-man-
agement" is replaced by a "new non-coercive method of management

. . . lead-management." In this philosophy, teachers and all others who work with students become lead-managers. According to Glasser,

> The leader is a facilitator in that he [*sic*] shows the workers that he has done everything possible to provide them with the best tools and workplace as well as a noncoercive, nonadversarial atmosphere in which to do the job.[18]

Throughout the book, Glasser cites Johnson City as an example of a district where administrators, teachers, and students have been trained to eliminate coercion from their lives and to ensure high levels of quality for all humans in the school.

How did the Johnson City of the 1970s, where there was a "rigorous wrestling for power" between the superintendent, school board, community, and teachers over the power of the district, develop into a "quality school" of noncoercive management? How did Champlin's bold, aggressive use of power during his superintendency become shared power where "everyone is a leader," where the "leaders become associates, associates become leaders"? How did the dialectical nature of power and knowledge in praxis mediate this transformation of leadership and work to turn the dancer into the dance and the dance into the dancer?

Champlin and Mamary's actions as superintendents over a twenty-year period portray the complex, dynamic interrelationship of knowledge and power. The actions of leaders such as Champlin and Mamary in schools and leaders such as George F. Johnson and Thomas J. Watson in corporations reveal the complexities of their ethical conduct within the cultures surrounding them. In their actions, their values and their knowledge of what Sarason calls the theoretical within the social-institutional context are dynamically combined, displayed, and interpreted by themselves and others. To understand more clearly the nature of the praxis of leadership as it occurred in the Johnson City schools during reform, let us filter it through the district's own conceptual framework and then through the writings of Freire, Kreisberg, and Foucault.

In the dissemination process of the Outcome-Driven Development Model, which began after the Joint Dissemination Review Panel of the National Diffusion Network validated Johnson City's instructional reforms in 1985, the superintendent at that time, Albert Mamary, and the central office articulated the four "critical questions" to judge the process of reform in ODDM'S *Success Connections.*[19] *The Success Connections* questions the goals, knowledge, beliefs, and actions of a school district seeking school improvement. When answered clearly and consistently, the questions will "produce a synergy that empowers everyone in your organization."[20] The four questions are

1. What do we want?
2. What do we know?
3. What do we believe?
4. What do we do?

Although they were framed fourteen years after the advent of reform in Johnson City, these four questions provide an excellent lens to view the process of reform in Johnson City from 1971 to the present and capture in a direct, simple form the Aristotelian conception of praxis as ethical conduct in a political context. In his moral theory of educational leadership, Hodgkinson stated that the meaning of "ethical" in this concept of praxis was a "commitment in advance" by the actor that extended beyond the "knowing in action" of Schon's reflective practioner.[21] This commitment to action by a leader or follower involved more than the "science"; it also encompassed human values—the intentions, the motives, the morals, and the emotions of the actor.

ODDM's four critical questions probe these aspects of praxis: "knowing" as the knowledge base from which one acts; "believing" as those statements that humans accept as true; "wanting" as the aspects of life that humans value; and, finally, "doing" as the commencement of an action in accordance with the commitment formed from reflection upon wanting, knowing, and believing.

The roots of the Johnson City district's answers to these critical questions lay in the history of the outer cultural ground, the outer "political context" of the district and community, as portrayed in the preceding chapters. The actual form of the district's answers is found in the inner layer of the social-institutional context where the "structure, the implicit and explicit rules, traditions, power relationships, and purposes are defined by its members."[22] This context includes all of those networks of power and knowledge within the schools, i.e, the relationships of teacher to administrator, teacher to teacher, teacher to student, administrator to student, student to student, and administrator to administrator, in addition to the relationships of these actors to the parents of children, the school-board members, and to the auxiliary service staff of secretaries, janitors, nurse, aides, etc. In this layer of schooling, the actors are characteristic of all schools regardless of size, geographical location, and financial support. While the outer cultural ground shapes the values of schooling, the analysis of this layer provides the strongest generalizations for the process of reform in other school districts.

Praxis occurs in these networks of power and knowledge at the microlevel of everyday political life in schools and is where authentic educational reform takes place. At this level, individuals in schools are either dominated by or empowered through the praxis of the theoretical and social-institutional context of schooling. Here is the power relationship among the individuals who constitute the "we" in the four questions of the *Success Connections* and where the justification of leadership occurs. The construction of the "we" establishes the relationship between leader and follower and whether this relationship is one of domination or empowerment for all individuals in the relationship.

Education has been presented as an act of domination in Paulo Freire's analysis of the teacher-student relationship in *Pedagogy of the Oppressed*. To conceptualize education as domination, Freire used the metaphor of banking:

> Education [is] . . . an act of depositing, in which the students are the depositories and the teacher is the depositor. In the banking concept of education, knowledge is a gift bestowed by those who consider themselves knowledgeable upon those whom they consider to know nothing. . . . the educator's role is to regulate the way the world "enters into" the students.[23]

By regulating the student's construction of reality to receive deposits of "true knowledge," the educator, knowingly or unknowingly, works to create "passive" recipients who will serve the purposes of the depositor, hopefully without questioning this reality. This act of the imposition of an externally conceived knowledge negates the consciousness of the recipient and works to oppress the individual into the existing order of the school.

According to Freire, education of this nature is "an exercise of domination . . . with the ideological intent . . . of indoctrinating [students] to adapt to the world of oppression."[24] Kreisberg expanded upon the exercise of power developed in Freire's banking metaphor to argue that the exercise of domination is the "dominant discourse of power in modern Western culture, which is reflected in our popular culture, in our institutions, throughout our social relations, and within the social sciences."[25]

In his analysis of the foundations of contemporary power theory, Kreisberg found that the most prominent interpretations of power in our culture conceived of power as a relationship of dominance and imposition, what Kreisberg calls "power over."[26] This conception of power is

> the ability to impose one's will on others as the means toward ful-
> filling one's desired goals. It is the ability to direct and control and
> to manipulate and coerce if need be, sometimes for the good of all,
> most often for the good of the few. Power is embodied in images
> of the father, the teacher, the political leader, the policeman, the
> soldier, and the businessman.[27]

Kreisberg also maintained that this conception of power in modern Western culture had an implicit assumption of inevitable tension and competition between "individual fulfillment and the needs and desires of other individuals and the community as a whole."[28] Drawing upon the work of Richard Katz, Kreisberg maintained that the assumption of conflict as an inherent element in "power over" in Western society is grounded in a paradigm of reality called the "scarcity paradigm." In the scarcity paradigm, humans construct reality through a belief that "resources are scarce; their presumed scarcity largely determines their value, [and] individuals or communities must compete with each other to gain access to these resources."[29]

When Jack Champlin began his superintendency, he stated that he arrived with a "clear message" for the implementation of an instructional program based upon individualized student mastery in the Johnson City schools. He immediately set out to "renorm" the school board, staff, and community to the principles of student mastery by "banking" this information into all members of the district through meetings and task force committees in what, as we saw, one resident called "brainwashing" sessions. According to Champlin,

> My message was direct and clear: I did not come to maintain your
> current program because it is substantially ineffective. It contra-
> dicts what we know about how young people learn best. . . .
> Business as usual was no longer acceptable. . . . I established a
> need to create a school environment far more consistent with best

available learning data . . . I accepted the need not only to deal aggressively with the professional staff but also to reeducate, renorm, and reactivate the entire community.[30]

Champlin's actions to impose his knowledge upon groups within his professional staff and in the outer community—his efforts to use "power over" these groups to implement his instructional program—led to a wrestling for power and repeated conflicts with staff members and community residents. Petitions to "oust him" from "disgusted residents," budget defeats, the replacement of incumbents who endorsed his programs by new board members who vowed to get "rid of Champlin," and union difficulties with the professional staff led by a disgruntled former football coach were weapons used to challenge Champlin. Each faction struggled against Champlin and his manifestations of "power over" to regain their power in the schools in a competition for the control of the district and the lives of the children, the families, and workers in this district.

Freire has argued that education should be an exercise of liberation, or empowerment. For Freire, "liberating education consist[s] in acts of cognition, not transferrals of information."[31] Education as liberation is "problem-posing" education, where the teacher is "no longer merely the one who teachs, but the one who is himself taught in dialogue with the students, who in turn while being taught also teach." Such education recognizes the consciousness within each individual and ensures that each person's construction of reality arises through authentic, free, active social interaction or dialogue with outside knowledge. "Problem-posing education bases itself on creativity and stimulates true reflection and action upon reality."[32]

Kreisberg explored these alternative notions of power in the writings of several theorists, including Erich Fromm, Rollo May, Jean Baker Miller, Starhawk, and Mary Parker Follett, which expose the limitations of a perspective of power viewed strictly as one of domination. Through his analysis of these other conceptualizations of power, Kreisberg arrived at an alternative conception termed "power with":

> Power with is manifest in *relationships of co-agency*. These relationships are characterized by people finding ways to satisfy their desires and to fulfill their interests without imposing on one another. The relationship of co-agency is one is which there is equality: situations in which individuals and groups fulfill their desires by acting together. It is

jointly developing capacity. The possibility for *power with*
lies in the reality of human interconnections within communities.[33]

In human communities where a conception of "power with"
exists, resources are created by "human activity and intention" where
the potential is intrinsically expanding and renewing. Such activities
include helping, healing, and learning. In contrast to a paradigm of
scarcity, this construction of reality is based in a paradigm of synergy.
"In synergistic communities valued resources are experienced as
accessible, expanding, and renewable, rather than scarce. Within synergistic communities, mechanisms and attitudes exist that guarantee
the equitable distribution of valued resources."[34] Within the synergy
paradigm, individuals in a community do not view themselves as
"possessors" of a valued resource, but rather as "guardians." These
guardians are motivated by a desire to help others in the community
and, therefore, will make efforts to share the resource with all others
in the community in an environment that encourages cooperation
rather than competition. The contradiction of the synergistic community lies in the effect that the more the valued "resource is utilized, the
more there is to be utilized."[35]

Kreisberg's alternative conception of power within a relationship
of coagency is illustrated in Champlin's use of power as a superintendent who directly involved himself in the instructional program of the
schools. In this role, Champlin was a team member with the teachers
who were implementing mastery learning. Immediately upon his
arrival, Champlin began working with a group of eight teachers in the
smallest elementary school in the district to implement strategies for
student mastery in their classrooms. These teachers had begun experimenting with student mastery in their individual classrooms prior to
Champlin's superintendency. They were the first teachers in the district to commit themselves to the practice of mastery learning and
under Champlin's direction began working in multigrade teams. The
nature of the relationship between Champlin and these teachers was
critically different from the one he enacted with all other groups in the
district. He recalled this early work with these teachers in this passage:

> I provided the initial training in brief after-school sessions and
> half-day released time blocks. Seeing their superintendent roll up
> his sleeves and actually work with them in training and problem
> solving was a totally new and stimulating experience for these

teachers. It established my credibility in terms of technical expertise. The district no longer had to go outside for consultant assistance. We had in-house power. . . . The teachers and I agreed that we would contribute equally so that each would have something at stake. The training began in a spirit of cooperativeness and mutuality.[36]

Champlin's relationship with this group of teachers was one of empowerment through which both superintendent and teachers were involved in mutual dialogue and shared work in a community to improve the learning of all of the children in their classrooms. This "equal" relationship of empowerment was qualitatively different from the "banking" relationship of dominance he imposed upon others through his "clear message" of the data-driven and goal-driven instructional process of mastery learning.

The relationship of coagency that shaped a conceptualization of power as "power with" in the district began with this group of teachers. Each year this relationship among teachers and administrators expanded through yearly, intensive summer training sessions for each new group of teachers who wanted to implement mastery learning in their classrooms. These sessions were conducted by teachers and administrators. Champlin and his assistant superintendent Albert Mamary also conducted ongoing in-service training with implementing teachers and principals throughout the year. Champlin recalled in his 1994 article,

The key to success was the professional staff. At Johnson City staff were neither encouraged nor permitted to move into the program until they were ready. Each staff member had the time and opportunity to personally "own" a pressing need for program improvement. The training sessions provided . . . the opportunity to think through and create a written philosophical premise that would establish a reason for all our instructional decision-making . . . [and] specific training was provided in every skill the new program required.[37]

The interrelationship of the knowledge and the research base of mastery learning and the use of "power with" by Champlin, Mamary, and other leaders in the district during the change process in the schools slowly led to the transformation of praxis within the district. As this occurred, a paradigm of synergy replaced the paradigm of scarcity. Within this transformation, Champlin's conception of power and his use of power was strongly affected by the political context of the situation and his conceptual paradigm of the human resources involved, as the preceding contrasting examples demonstrate.

The dynamic interrelationship of knowledge and power conceptualized in Michel Foucault's writings provides a framework to understand the transformation of the praxis in the Johnson City schools by both Champlin and the teachers in these early years. Their successful interrelationships to implement instructional strategies for students created jointly developed facilities within all of them. The synergy of this "power with" began slowly to infuse other relationships these actors had in schooling.

Foucault has argued that power imbues all relationships and experiences among humans who engage in any form of social action. Foucault perceives power, however, not as a top-down movement but as a capillary action in a series of human networks and relationships. The humans in these relationships may or may not even be aware of power's exercise in their interactions. Power can be repressive or positive in its effects as it promotes pleasure as well as constitutes humans as subjects in various ways.[38] Foucault reasons that a relationship of power "is a mode of action which does not act directly and immediately on others . . . [but] instead it acts upon their actions . . . on existing actions and on those which may arise in the present or in the future."[39]

Arguing that power and knowledge are inextricably linked, Foucault presents them as one concept: "power/knowledge." He observes that "the exercise of power perpetually creates knowledge and, conversely, knowledge constantly induces effects of power."[40] Foucault maintains that knowledge and power are joined in "discourse . . . as a group of statements that belong to a single system of formation." Discourse exists "whenever a pattern of regularity or a complex group of relations that function as a rule exist between statements, objects, or concepts."[41] In a discourse, there are "rules for particular statements to be made, how particular concepts are used, and how particular strategies are used."[42] This discourse then determines the underlying rules for both what and how things can be said as well as who can speak and who must listen. The dominant discourse of a practice is thereby defined by those in authority and affects the fundamental understanding of this practice by those who are in the relationship.

As Champlin and the teachers in the Oakdale elementary school saw their students achieve at higher levels through the practice of mastery learning, Champlin continually refined the district's understanding of these instructional strategies through meetings and in-services. Through the ongoing articulation of the philosophy and principles of mastery learning by Champlin, teachers, parents, board members, and a growing number of people in the district, mastery learning became the dominant discourse of instructional practice in Johnson City.

Although internal documentation of district reports do not substantiate Champlin's statements regarding a "clear message" of mastery learning in 1971, Champlin did arrive in Johnson City with knowledge of Bloom's Learning for Mastery and a commitment to its implementation in the district. This knowledge formed the basis of his expert power with the school board, the teachers, and the community. To establish the discourse of mastery learning, Champlin established regular opportunities for board members, teachers, and community members to come to know "the rules" for statement of this philosophy, how the particular concepts of mastery learning were to be constructed, and how particular strategies of mastery learning were to be used in the district during the first two years of his superintendency.

By 1973 at the recommendation of Champlin and district task forces, the Johnson City school board formally adopted an instructional policy, "The Learning Environment Goal." This policy codified the district's commitment to creating an "optimum personalized learning environment for each pupil."[43] This policy stated that structure and implementation of the program would be based upon "valid, substantiated learning data," include "continuous assessment for renewal and restructure," and have "effective management."[44] Champlin stated that the policy

> was a bold and courageous step for the board to take, considering the community's past views of school and the nature of learning. To my knowledge, this public policy was the first of this nature in the country. The policy became a powerful weapon. It enabled me to initiate a much larger purpose and mission.[45]

As Champlin later recognized, the policy was a weapon of the knowledge/power relationship. This policy formalized the educational process, gave formal justification to Champlin's leadership, and further empowered the dominant discourse of mastery learning as a data-driven system to transform the district. Champlin used the policy as an effective means to put formal power behind his efforts to corral teachers and parents into accepting the instructional changes. He revisited the policy during the yearly reorganization of the board as a means of using this discourse to guide the actions of all within the district. He also used this policy to guide the instructional goals for the district in the coming year. In a sense, Champlin used the discourse of mastery learning as an ever-widening mesh of forms and meanings that he integrated into people's language, beliefs, and actions about schools.

In the everyday political life of schools, power operates at an almost unconscious level; the dominant discourse operates through agents such as Champlin and teachers who are adopting the instructional process of mastery learning. Foucault insisted that this power cannot be violent in the sense of an act of force or coercion, but requires that the person upon whom it is exercised is "thoroughly recognized and maintained to the very end as a person who acts."[46] In the knowledge/power relationship the coagent, the follower, must be free to act and have before him or her "a whole variety of responses, reactions, results, and possible inventions."

Resistance to the knowledge/power discourse, as Foucault noted, remains one of the responses available to the coagent.

> We must make allowance for the complex and unstable process whereby discourse can be both an instrument and effect of power, but also a hindrance, a stumbling-block, a point of resistance and a starting point for an opposing strategy.[47]

Such resistance to Champlin's discourse on instruction began six months into his first year as superintendent. Community members soundly defeated his proposal for a new middle school referendum; the union called for the school board to reject the hiring of Albert Mamary as Champlin's assistant superintendent. Coagent resistance to Champlin persisted until his retirement in 1982. Budget defeats, incumbent defeats, petitions to oust him as superintendent, teacher grievances, student walkouts, irate community members, and letters to the editors were the most visible forms of resistance from the community and teaching staff.

Champlin's responses to this resistance were again complex and multidimensional. He exercised "power over" through his use of expert knowledge to influence the community and through his use of various incentives and punishments to coerce resisting professional staff. Although these actions generally quelled the immediate disturbance, the anger, resentment, and resistance went underground and waited for the next opportunity to blow up in his face. At the same time he was attacking and being ambushed by various segments of the staff and community, he continued to work in a "power with" relationship with his coagents: the staff, teachers, and parents first at Oakdale and then in the other schools that began the implementation of mastery learning. As these people worked with Champlin and observed increased student achievement through their efforts, they became active agents in the discourse of mastery learning. In the ten-year period of 1971 through 1981, these coagents and their discourse became the most effective means of overcoming those who were resistant to the educational changes.

In addition, his own enactment of the discourse of mastery learning via the mediation of the shared work and "problem-posing" mutual dialogue of his direct contact with teachers and board members transformed his own praxis. As Champlin worked with his staff, his construction of the knowledge/power relationship changed. In a dialectical nature, the coagency of his relationship of power with the implementing teachers and staff members working within the discourse of mastery learning revealed the inherent contradictions of his actions of "power over." As stated by Carr and Kemmis in their description of dialectical thinking,

> As contradictions are revealed, new constructive thinking and new constructive action are required to transcend the contradictory state of affairs. The complementarity of the elements is dynamic: it is a kind of a tension, not a static confrontation between the two poles.[48]

By establishing a dominant discourse of learning that did not fall within a paradigm of scarcity and by enacting a "power with" relationship of liberation, Champlin and the staff of Johnson City began to reconceive and reconstruct their district within a paradigm of synergy and began the process of transforming the leader into the associate, the associate into the leader, the dancer into the dance, the dance into the dancer.

7

Outlawing the Bell-Shaped Curve

If knowledge is our primary power, then one acquires influence by being a continuous learner, one committed to act on best knowledge once mastered.

—John R. Champlin

In his eleven years as superintendent of the Johnson City Schools, Champlin formed with his administrative staff and teachers a process critical to the implementation and sustainability of the educational changes that led to ODDM. He began by establishing a "clear message" of educational improvement for the district and demonstrated that he "intended to take appropriate risks to effect program improvement." In his personal retrospective on the district's reform over twenty years later, Champlin recollected that he then "introduced two terms critical to [his] value and belief system: goal-driven and data-driven."[1] With these two terms, Champlin defined a process by which all decisions and actions within the district would be made.

All practices within the schools were to be driven by the goals of the district and by the best research and knowledge available to teachers and administrators. Any instructional practice that was not in alignment with these goals and data would not be supported by the administration, should be discontinued, and should be replaced with practices that supported the goals and reflected "best knowledge."

This process of instructional alignment with goals and research continuously served to shape the dominant discourse of the district until almost all people in the organization were coagents in the discourse and all formal programs were aligned with this discourse. Through the instructional alignment of the educational practices in the Johnson City Schools, kindergarten through grade twelve, the interconnected relationship of knowledge/power as characterized by Foucault was formed. Instructional alignment herded teachers, staff, and students into the rules, strategies, and concepts that drove the overall system and worked to acculturate them into the belief system, language, and culture of mastery learning as the dominant discourse. This chapter illustrates the alignment of instructional practices with the goals and data of the district and the modes of power Champlin used as superintendent to bring almost all facets of the educational system into agreement.

As defined by Champlin, the first of the two terms, *goal-driven,* "conveyed the intention that every professional action or decision worked toward our published goal: all children learning well what schools taught." All instructional practices in support of this published goal were "*data-driven,*" i.e., they were derived from the research base and had to be "consistent with the best available learning data."[2]

This goal-driven process for screening every instructional decision made in the district did not necessarily inhibit innovative practices, but it ensured that any proposal for a new educational strategy or program had to align with the district's core belief that all children had unlimited learning capacity. Having studied the process of change and systems theory as part of his doctoral work, Champlin held the belief that the school district was an interconnected and interdependent "ecological system [where] alterations and changes in one part of the system will have reciprocal impact on the balance of the whole system."[3]

For Champlin, the heart of this ecological system, the pump through which all parts of the system flowed and were connected, was Johnson City's basic philosophical premise, which originated in Bloom's Learning for Mastery instructional strategy: "Under the right conditions, almost all students are capable of achieving excellence in learning."

Champlin fervently believed that all actions within a school system had to align to effect meaningful change. To establish a "total, cohesive organizational effort," every part of the organization had to embrace and respond to any new practice. In the following example taken from the effective school research literature, Champlin illustrated how data from the effective schools literature could be misused within a school district if the conditions for increased student achievement were not aligned with all other parts of the organization:

> While the Effective Schools Movement has provided a service in reminding schools that the product will be enhanced when these conditions are in place, there has been an approximate reciprocal disservice by not reminding users that alterations must be connected and managed intentionally to ensure an alignment with all other parts of the organization. A district/building typically selects 2–3 characteristics and then invests several years in their development. The result often has been that there are three altered conditions, each of which has not had intentional connectedness with other critical parts of the organization.[4]

Alignment of instruction to effect student achievement occurred only through "intentional" management and connection with all other parts. Champlin's beliefs regarding the change process and the role of the "change agent" or leader in effecting educational improvement clearly entailed "intention," or in Hodgkinson's words, conscious commitment to act within the political context of schools as the praxis of moral leadership. A leader consciously defined the beliefs and knowledge that would shape the overt practices of all those working within the system.

In Johnson City, all parts of the instructional system were connected and aligned with the core belief of mastery learning during the two decades of Champlin and Mamary's superintendencies. By outlawing the application of the image of the bell-shaped curve's distribution of student aptitude to the distribution of student achievement, they worked to deconstruct the scarcity paradigm that had governed the Johnson City schools, like most American schools, since the beginning of the twentieth century. Creating a new pattern for understanding student achievement as an ever-expanding resource, the philosophical premise of mastery worked to connect all parts of the educational organization and to shift Johnson City's administrative and teaching staff's construction of reality from American education's dominant scarcity paradigm to a paradigm of synergy. As defined by Katz, the premise of mastery learning acted as a synergistic pattern:

A synergistic pattern brings phenomena together, interrelating them, creating a new and greater whole from the disparate parts. In that pattern phenomena exist in harmony with each other maximizing each other's potential. Two phrases capture this quality: "The whole is greater than sum of the parts," and "What is good for one is good for all."[5]

In an educational system based on mastery learning, learning was not a finite resource but was unlimited, allowing the potential of every student to be maximized and not regulated by a belief in the random distribution of intelligence. The successful achievement of one student did not hinge upon the failure of another student; all had the opportunity to achieve. Current ODDM materials routinely depict this simple but powerful synergistic pattern in the following logo:

Fig. 2. Logo used by Partners for Quality Learning/ODDM. Reprinted with permission by the National Center for Outcome Based Education, 1993.

The potential performance level for every student within the new system of the Outcomes-Driven Developmental Model is represented by the figure which follows. As indicated in the new learning curve, the ODDM system will boost 50 percent of student test scores to a high performance level.

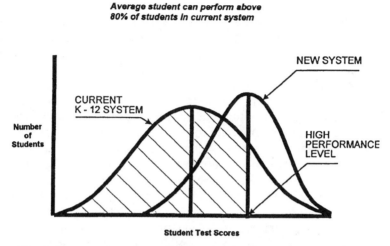

Fig. 3. Reprinted with permission from the National Center for Outcome Based Education, 1993.

All decision making in the district was to begin with this premise and its emphasis upon increases in achievement for each student. The alignment of instructional practices through a goal-driven process, however, did not occur overnight, but was long and gradual. By 1977, all teachers and principals in the elementary schools and the middle school were involved in an instructional process directed to the goals of the district to some extent. The children who entered first grade in 1977 became the first group in the district to proceed through each grade level to graduation in 1989 in programs framed on this core philosophy.

As educational practices changed to interconnect with this philosophy, the dominant discourse of mastery learning worked to transform the praxis of the teachers, the parents, the school-board members, and administrative staff in these buildings, as well as the children who were engaged in this new approach to their learning capacity.

Summer training sessions, in-services throughout the school year, parent meetings, staff meetings, parent surveys and newsletters, community and staff task-force meetings, and the meetings of the school board began with a goal-driven process to enact the discourse of mastery learning. Champlin consistently began sessions with the professional staff, the school board, and the community with the core belief of the district. He also worked extensively with the professional staff to write curricular documents that supported this belief during the summer in-service training sessions and task-force meetings on the redesign of the school district. Board meetings also provided him the opportunity to establish the primacy of the district goals. For example, in October 1976 he introduced the "challenge of redesign for the total school environment" to board members, outlining the activities of the upcoming superintendent's conference day in which elementary and secondary staff would initiate total school redesign and produce an acceptable definition of quality education within the district.

The forthcoming document stated the goals of the district as the preparation of a curriculum that would accommodate the "future needs of society by ensuring each learner an active role in the learning process and progress at a rate commensurate with his/her ability." To accomplish those "exit behaviors in students" which defined a "quality education . . . total involvement of the board, administration, staff, and parents" in this task would be necessary.[6]

Champlin's strategies to align people and programs with the district's goals often involved risk, as this example indicates. In 1974 Champlin and Mamary outlined for the board the objectives and results of a program whereby the elementary administrators of the district had exchanged schools for a week.[7] The report noted that

> For an administrator to live in another administrator's building for a week, to see what another administrator has done and to share openly with staff his perceptions is a very high risk activity but highly beneficial to all.[8]

Mamary explained to the board the objectives that he had negotiated with each administrator before the exchange. Each administrator needed to decide what he wanted to learn, act as a change agent and offer help to the teams in the building, assess the staff and program, and share with the visiting school's staff his own observations and perceptions. One of the key questions in this assessment was, "Is the staff actually doing what they said they wanted to do?"[9] This strategy not only revealed compliance or noncompliance with the goals and exerted pressure on all to conform, but also established a means for the sharing of knowledge and action and for the connecting of all parts of the ecological system.

During the 1977 school year Champlin and Mamary moved the program improvement to the high school, where they, the high school principal, and a group of high school teachers developed a redesigned instructional program for the high school aligned with the philosophical premises of mastery learning. The "Program Redesign" report, adopted by the school board in March 1977, outlined a program of "total staff involvement" to bring the professional staff to a close working relationship with the existing "District Philosophy" for personalized learning, and outlined a total restructuring of the instructional process to align with Bloom's Learning for Mastery model. The report limned a secondary program designed to "emphasize basic skill attainment . . . and to establish college expectations" in a community where college attendance had traditionally been reserved for the children of its more affluent, elite members of the community.[10]

Of the district's teaching staff, the high school teachers had exhibited the strongest resistance to the district's discourse. A 1980 article on mastery learning and Johnson City in the *New York Times* noted this resistance. An interview with a high school teacher reveals the pressure of Champlin's leadership:

> Armed with the successes of mastery learning in the elementary and middle schools, Dr. Champlin is now pressing a reluctant high school faculty to adopt the method. Although the superintendent said he preferred an "evolutionary approach to a revolutionary one," a number of high school teachers said they now feel increased pressure to move from their more traditional method of teaching.
>
> "Champlin has installed a 'personal growth file' to encourage the district's 185 teachers to pick up new mastery-learning skills, [and] develop a new job description that reflects the use of these skills, and has made it clear to all prospective teachers that the mastery approach is a must," said one high school teacher. "Like the system or not, we really don't have much choice in the matter. When the administrator comes by your classroom and asks, 'Where are you in the instructional process?' you better be able to tell him."[11]

Champlin's use of power to establish the discourse of mastery learning was multidimensional and complex. With staff who were motivated to become coagents in discourse of mastery learning and willing to implement the practice, or who had already been implementing aspects of the practice in their classrooms, Champlin's use of power was coactive in that he shared power as a means to initiate "best knowledge" and to shape the practices of instruction in a form of "power with." With those who had no knowledge of the discourse, and especially with those who resisted the implementation of the dominant discourse in the district, he used assertive, coercive power to dominate these people and force changes in their educational practices with students; thus his use of the above-mentioned "personal growth file," which was used to assess the performance of teachers and administrators in the district.

Champlin exercised power coercively as "power over" during most of his tenure at Johnson City. He dominated groups with his expert knowledge or used the psychological and material rewards and punishments at his disposal as superintendent to establish staff compliance in the use of mastery learning in classrooms and to garner parental, school board, and community support of these strategies. Champlin overcame staff resistance to the dominant discourse and to the pressure for instructional alignment by encouraging the retirement of resisting personnel or their transfer to a neighboring school district. Other staff members found themselves pulled into the discourse and to ostensible compliance by Champlin's barrage of knowledge on the practice, pressure from colleagues, participation in year-round training sessions, and the evaluation process of the administration. Parents were also actively pulled into the planning of the curriculum and redesign of the district's buildings through task forces.

The community was not so easily subjected to Champlin's knowledge/power and continued to assert its own resistance at the ballot box. In response to the petitions and budget defeats, Champlin conducted annual surveys of parental assessment of the programs, which consistently ranked the educational changes as positive and declared their satisfaction with its effects upon their children. But Champlin's antagonistic, "power over" relationship with certain segments of the outer community and the teachers' association continued. Annual budgets were still being defeated through his last years in the district. In 1980 two new board members were elected on the basis of their public attacks on Champlin's leadership. Champlin's enduring acrimonious relationship with the leadership of the teachers' association also prolonged contract negotiations through 1979 and 1980, revealing the bitter conflicts that were still festering from the early days of Champlin's leadership and the teachers' strike that had been barely averted in 1976.

Although he remained locked into coercive power struggles with segments of the community and his teaching staff, he was able to use coactive power with those administrators, teachers, parents, and board members who did not resist or, in the best scenario, believed in the power of the discourse of mastery learning.

For example, his success in working with district teachers to change practice within each school, and with using the district's own teaching and administrative staff to train faculty rather than hire outside consultants, led to his recommendation in 1979 of a board-adopted policy on staff development. In this policy the board committed ongoing funds for staff growth and material in exchange for the staff's commitment to use professional literature and to develop personal growth files to assess professional competence and renewal.

The alignment of faculty, staff, and community with the goals of the district through the discourse of mastery learning and later outcome-based education continued through the superintendency of Mamary. Although the district by this time had achieved overt agreement with the goals, covert resistance remained.

When such resistance was discovered, Mamary utilized both the knowledge of the goals and the process of the "Success Connections" to align beliefs and practices. For example, in the mid-1980s Mamary discovered that a team of teachers in one of the elementary schools was still putting children in ability groups and leaving them there all year long. During a two-day summer workshop, the superintendent and assistant superintendent spent these two days with the team of three teachers, working through the four questions of the "Success Connections." They went through each question, asking the teachers to respond and explain their beliefs. From here they went on to student exit behaviors, school policies, and classroom practices. By the end of the session, the teachers acknowledged the inconsistencies of their practices with district beliefs and policies and talked excitedly about what they would change when school opened in the fall.

After the session, Mamary chided the school principal for allowing the previous practices to occur in the first place and for taking so long to find out about them. He instructed the principal to spend a half-day at the beginning of the next school year with these teachers to go over again the beliefs and practices. The principal also was told to spend half an hour a day during the first few weeks with the team to help them get on the right track.[12] Mamary's use of power with its elements of "power over" and "power with" created knowledge /

power and firmly planted the dominant discourse of the district into this team's behaviors.

In addition to a goal-driven alignment of curriculum and instruction with the core belief of the district, Champlin used data, or as he called it, "best knowledge," to drive the system and to shape the discourse. This data included external research in the reform literature and internal data on student achievement, teaching practices, and parental assessments.

The first record of Champlin's use of data as knowledge/power is found in the school-board minutes of spring 1972, when a group of residents "opened fire" on Champlin's program. Presenting a petition to the board, the residents demanded that the "new program . . . in Oakdale Elementary School be submitted to the voters in a referendum."[13]

In the two-week period before the next board meeting, Champlin and his staff conducted a survey measuring parental response to the new program. The questionnaire was distributed to 565 families in three of the elementary schools, 520 of whom responded. Champlin presented the findings to the board that 81 percent approved of the district's efforts to "personalize the program" and supported the district's departure from the "traditional self-contained classroom situation."[14] As a result of the survey and Champlin's forceful recommendations, the board voted to reject the petition and restated their full support of his programs. Both Champlin and Mamary would continue to use district-designed surveys of the community to claim popular support for their programs.

The first report on student achievement data appeared in October 1973, two years into Champlin's superintendency. At this time, Champlin reported that the median scores of the district's elementary students in the third and sixth grades as measured on New York's PEP tests were higher than the median scores for all of the state's pupils, although not as high as the scores for the pupils in Broome County.[15]

The most comprehensive compilation of internal data on student achievement began in 1978 when Champlin and his staff prepared an exhaustive report for the school board detailing test data analysis that documented student achievement.[16] A comparison of student achievement scores on the New York Pupil Evaluation Program (PEP) tests in 1972 and 1977 in grades 3 and 6 for reading and math showed that the percentage of students in the district scoring at the lowest stanines had decreased, while the percentage of students in the highest stanines had increased significantly. In a comparison of the district percentages in each of the three stanine groupings, 7–9, 4–6, and 1–3, the percentage of Johnson City students in the top stanine in 1972 was considerably lower for grades 3 and 6 in reading and math. The fall 1977 percentages for the top stanine had increased for grade 3 reading and math and had exceeded the county percentages for grade 6 in reading and math. Champlin attributed the success of the district to the effectiveness of the mastery-learning program.

At the same meeting, Champlin used test data from student performances on the Regents examinations and the Scholastic Aptitude Tests to target the high school's poor performance in preparing students for college. The IBM school board, whose middle-class aspirations for their children included a college education, took special note of these inadequacies. The report criticized high school staff members' lowered expectations of students in the district and urged an "aggressive program of staff development" for the high school as recommended by the redesign task force.[17]

Having prepared a strong case for the restructuring of the high school program, Champlin easily gained the board's support to align the high school program with the core philosophy of mastery learning and to implement school improvement from kindergarten through twelfth grade.[18]

Champlin also worked with the board and staff to assess the postsecondary activities of Johnson City graduates and to develop an instructional program that would boost the educational and career choices of the district's graduates. Their survey confirmed the tenuous legacy of George F. Johnson and his disdain for a college education, revealing that a majority of Johnson City students did not continue their education beyond high school. Of the 49 percent who did attend a postsecondary institution, three-quarters enrolled in two-year institutions. To increase the number of students who aspired to four-year colleges, Champlin and his staff immediately implemented a new reading program with a strong emphasis on vocabulary and enriched reading and writing, as well as district SAT preparation courses, advanced placement courses, and summer enrichment courses. They also emphasized the responsibility of all learners to engage in enrichment and individual research projects. Because of the cohesiveness Champlin had established with administrative and teaching staff to implement change in instruction, the number of students who received the highly competitive New York Regents Scholarships tripled in the next two years.

Champlin's use of internal student achievement data to document the success of mastery learning enhanced professional staff receptivity to this instructional discourse and encouraged staff to participate in the program and to change their teaching practices in accordance with the district's goals, beliefs, and strategies. The district's significant increases in student achievement performances also attracted national attention. As recorded in the 1980 *Times* article:

> For a decade, mastery learning has been gradually injected into the city's school district. . . . It is the core ingredient in the Board of Education's philosophy and it is the single reason Dr. Champlin cites for the improvement of pupil performance in the 2,950-student district.[19]

The article recorded additional improvement on the New York State PEP tests and included statistics on student performance on the nationally normed California Achievement Tests:

> Test scores also bear testament to the achievements of students who, as a body, have an average I.Q. of 103. On the 1980 California Achievement Tests for reading and math, for example, first-graders were shown to be achieving at a full grade above their grade level, fifth-graders scored a grade and a half above their level, and eighth-graders achieved nearly three grades above their level.[21]

Additional national attention focused upon the school district in March 1981 when *Family Circle* magazine ran a feature article on "a revolutionary new teaching technique . . . called Mastery Learning" and its implementation in the Johnson City schools.[22] In the text of this article, the importance of the power/knowledge of Foucault's conceptualization of discourse is revealed:

> The secret behind mastery learning is the positive assumption it makes about children's capacity to learn. Given enough time, its proponents say, 95% of the children in school today can master *any* given subject—learn it well enough, that is, to deserve an A. . . . Dr. John Champlin . . . explains: "With mastery comes a whole different perspective on how kids relate to school. As they enjoy success, they develop very positive feelings toward schools; they *want* to attend.[22]

In the article, Champlin admitted, however, that full compliance or coagency with the discourse still had not been accomplished and that resistance among faculty and parents existed.

> Most Johnson City teachers say they wouldn't go back to a conventional program, with it's [sic] conventional assumptions about the "normal" distribution of ability amoung [sic] children, under any circumstances. However, a few teachers—and a few parents—were uncomfortable with the new system, so several classrooms in each school have been set aside for them, and in those classrooms something like the old system prevails. It's necessary, says Dr. Champlin, to "internalize" the philosophy of mastery learning in order to use it effectively, and he's aware that not everyone can do that.[23]

In Champlin's words, the "internalization" of the philosophy required the teacher, the parent, and the child to abandon a construction of reality within a paradigm of scarcity and to adopt the belief that human learning was unlimited and available to *all* children, a difficult challenge to individuals in a competitive society grounded in the principles of scarcity and of life as a zero-sum game.

The internalization of the discourse of mastery learning as well as his own exercise of coactive power also worked to reconstruct Champlin's understanding of power and changed his own practice. In his relationships with others in the organization, his exercise of coactive power increased, resulting in his retrospective upon the changes within Johnson City over a decade later, in which he conceptualized this meaning of power as "leader-associate" in a school district where "every person can be a leader."

The internalization of this philosophy by the staff and community of the Johnson City schools coalesced into the integrated principle Dewey claimed as the source of the "public" in his work on social democracy. This principle ultimately organized all elements of the district's educational system in the process of instructional alignment and, in doing so, created a whole learning community that was greater than the sum of its parts. The integrated principle of mastery learning supported, fed, and shaped an ethos of the common good within Johnson City which had not existed in the community since the halcyon days of Endicott Johnson's Square Deal. By sustaining the learning potential of all students in the system through the twelve years of schooling, the principle worked to ensure an equitable distribution of

the educational benefits of the community and to create an interrelationship of human effort and shared work in the accomplishment of
the common good.

8

Leading

Enough, if something from our hands have
*   power*
To live, and act, and serve the future hour;
And if, as toward the silent tomb we go,
Through love, through hope, and faith's transcen-
*   dent dower,*
We feel that we are greater than we know.
                    —William Wordsworth,
                        "The River Duddon,
                            After-Thought"

The districtwide commitment to the philosophy of mastery learning in the Johnson City schools, the data on student achievement that justified this commitment, and the continuous emphasis on using "best knowledge" to inform practice shaped the substance of the discourse of "truth" in the power relationships established under the leadership of both Champlin and Mamary. Their power, as Foucault argued, could not be exercised "without the production, accumulation, circulation and functioning of a discourse," and dialectically, this discourse could only be produced through the exercise of power. Foucault stated, "We are subjected to the production of truth through power and we cannot exercise power except through the production of truth."[1]

As leaders of the school district, both Champlin and Mamary used their power to operationalize the discourse of mastery learning that concurrently empowered them and all others in their relationships of power to develop a community of synergy. A sense of unity formed where the whole was greater than the sum of its parts, and as in Wordsworth's poem, the district formed a "we" who felt "we are greater than we know."

Champlin's retirement from the district in 1982 and Albert Mamary's succession as superintendent provided the opportunity for power as a coactive relationship or "power with" to become the dominant mode of power within the district. Community and staff conflicts with Champlin, who recalled that he felt "chastised for aspiring to a 'Cadillac' when the community was content with a used 'Ford,'" disappeared with Champlin's exit.[2] The same school-board members who had struggled with Champlin for the outer, political control of the district and had felt demeaned by Champlin's comments about their community immediately gave their support to Mamary.

As Champlin's assistant superintendent from 1972 to 1982, Mamary had worked under Champlin in a relationship that Champlin described as "Mutt and Jeff." Champlin perceived his role as one of "going into a meeting, shaking people up through ideas, and leaving. Mamary's job was to calm people down and encourage them to do what needed to be done."[3] During this first stage of instructional reform, Champlin and Mamary comprised what Lightfoot has termed the "professional marriage" of complementary styles, a "good guy–bad guy" relationship of intimacy and trust that, when combined, creates strong, consistent leadership.[4]

Under Champlin's tutelage, Mamary had established himself as a knowledgeable coleader who facilitated the process of change through cooperation and nurturance. School-board members viewed his personality as "pleasing" and "involved"; and Mamary was seen as a "yes man" who was "well-liked by all" and "able to handle the community."[5]

Throughout this stage, Mamary had consistently exhibited a conception of power that did not challenge the community; instead he shared his power with other people in the organization, including his administrative staff, teachers, parents, board members, community, and students. With Mamary's superintendency, this alternative form of power began to characterize all relationships within the district, and dynamically, a discourse on this conceptualization of power developed. The concepts, rules, and strategies of this discourse further legitimatized this alternative conception of power and determined the underlying assumptions for the use of power between administrators and teachers, between teachers and students, and within all networks of power in the inner layer of the social-institutional context of schooling.

As we examine the second decade of the commitment to educational reform in Johnson City, we ask, how did this discourse take shape and frame an alternative conception of power? Was Mamary's leadership and his exercise of coactive power sufficient to establish the discourse? Or did other forms of knowledge also work to establish it? The next two chapters examine more fully the meaning of coactive power, its application within the Johnson City schools, and the development of a discourse on this power within a synergistic community.

Mary Parker Follett maintained that the use of coercive power would be reduced in an organization where coactive power was prevalent. The process of sharing power and arriving jointly at a solution that embraced all the needs of all the interests involved "creative integration," according to Follett. Creative integration was "a technique of human relationship based upon the preservation of the integrity of the individual."[6]

As explained by Nancy Smith in her exploration of Follett's writings and their implications for educational leaders, Follett believed conflict was not only inevitable but desirable.[7] Conflicts in opinions, experiences, and interests had a "plus value" in that they added to the variety of perspectives on the problem at hand and to the breadth of the issue at the root of the conflict. The resolution of the conflict between these views, opinions, and experiences through domination by one member or faction, or through compromise in which both sides lost something, was flawed in that the conflict eventually occurred again. More importantly, domination or compromise limited the construction of reality regarding the solution to a win-loss situation, a zero-sum game: if one member won, the other lost; in compromise, if one gave up something, then the other also gave up something.

Follett stated that creative integration involved the "intention of a solution in which the desires of all parties are not sacrificed but all 'win.'"[8] In creative integration, the individuals involved in the conflict worked through understanding and participation to create a new solution incorporating the wants of all involved to the agreement of all and in doing so, progress resulted. The dialectical nature of the process, in turn, changed the situation and so the process began again at a higher level. Creative integration raised the conflict to a higher level, which Follett viewed as progress. Follett stated, "Social progress is in this respect like individual progress; we become spiritually more and more developed as our conflicts rise to higher levels."[9]

In the integrative process, according to Follett, there is "reciprocal influence," as experienced by Champlin and the first group of teachers who were implementing mastery learning. Here, there are many members of the group acting through several networks of relationship and contributing and responding dynamically and simultaneously. From reciprocal influence, "emergence" occurs and new solutions, new values, new capacities, and more power are created. According to Follett, "Synthesis and creation [is] achieved in the process of circular influencing."[10] In this process a synergistic pattern forms and a unity is created:

> all parts [are] so coordinated, so moving together in their closely knit and adjusting activities, so linking, interlocking, interrelating, that they make a working unit. . . . what I have called a functional whole or integrative unity.[11]

Follett believed that the coactive power of leader and associate in creative integration respected the differences of interests so as not to blur identity, but it eliminated fighting. Smith termed this process as "getting to yes," where those interests involved generated a solution that provided for the needs of all in the organization.[12]

From her work in *Creative Experience*, Follett continued to explore this conceptualization of power within the framework of administration and organization in writings that were compiled by a friend in the book *Dynamic Administration* after Follett's death.[13] In these papers, which Follett had requested to be destroyed, she focused upon a leader's constructive meaning of control in organizations and also articulated four fundamental principles of organization. Smith claimed that Follett "conceived of control as the result of integration" and as a "desirable outcome for all individuals and the group."[14] Gaining constructive control in an organization was accomplished through "fact-control" rather than through the control of people in the organization and resulted from the "correlation of many points of power, a collective control, rather than from a 'super-imposed control.'"[15]

In her four fundamental principles of organization, which are listed below, Follett viewed the processes of constructive leadership and control as providing an "interpenetration" of all parts of the organization through coordination. These four principles are

1. Coordination by direct contact of the responsible people concerned;
2. Coordination in the early stages;
3. Coordination as the reciprocal relating of all the factors in a situation;
4. Coordination as a continuing process.[16]

Follett believed that the continuous process of "coordinating" all parts of the organization would establish a dynamic form of organization that was in an ongoing state of renewal and regeneration to higher and higher levels. Her work on coactive power and constructive leadership is an important framework for understanding the leadership of Mamary and the continuous process of renewal in the Johnson City schools.

Mamary began his superintendency with major goals that reflected his conception of power as coactive, cooperative, and reciprocal and included statements such as "be sensitive to public and community, improve staff morale, build coalitions to get the job done, and improve the home-school relationship."[17] These goals reveal his emphasis upon the importance of interrelationships of schooling and the need to connect the major players who supported the learning of students. Mamary's conceptualization of power as a coactive relationship continued through his years as superintendent, 1982–93. In a retrospective of his leadership of the district and the development of ODDM, Mamary credited the success of the district and of the ODDM process to these relationships of power, which he perceived as partnership:

> [S]uccess comes from the kind of environment you create. We started by trying to create an environment where everybody was considered in partnership with the operation.
> The Johnson City schools live by three principles. Here's the first one: all staff members will be involved in every major decision. The second idea is that we will always strive for 100 percent agreement, even if we have to go back many times. And third, we have an agreement that everybody will live by the agreements until we change them—and agreements should be changed now and then.
> Back in 1972, I said a position in this district is not power. Instead, we said knowledge is power, using knowledge is power. We said—and we meant it—that we are coworkers and co-learners and co-doers. And I think that is why the district is where it is today.[18]

Mamary's first principle reflects this conceptualization of shared power, of "power with," where every staff member is involved in the making of major decisions. The second principle describes the process of creative integration Follett recommended, whereby the solutions to conflicts and differences over issues or strategies are worked cooperatively until all agree and are satisfied with the results. The coordination she postulated in the four fundamental principles of organization manifested itself very early in the reform of Johnson City's schooling through Champlin's idea of schooling as an ecological system, with each part coordinated with the every other part to create an integrated whole. As the facilitator of the actions within the district, Mamary used primarily coactive power to fuel this coordination in his work with teachers, parents, the school board, administrators, community, and students. Mamary realized, as did Follett, that this agreement entailed conflict, and possibly several sessions of circular influencing, before a creative solution emerged from the process that incorporated the wants of all involved and contributed to an increasing sense of power for all.

One anecdote often used by Mamary, staff, and a former school-board president illustrates the district's process of creative integration with staff, parents, and students. Because of the district's prohibition against smoking, students would gather in their cars during their lunch break in a parking lot farthest away from the high school building. Disruptive incidents among students frequently occurred during this time, often requiring administrative intervention and resulting in disciplinary actions. After several meetings with students on this problem, the staff agreed with the students to designate the southern courtyard adjacent to the school an area for student smoking. The proximity to the building resulted in fewer and fewer disruptive incidents. A couple of months after this solution had been instituted to the satisfaction of both students and staff, the students asked for the school's official recognition of the group as a club and requested a faculty advisor. The students named their club the "Southies" and began various community fund-raising and volunteer projects that, in turn, changed the negative perceptions of their group held by the school and community into positive ones. Although there was no change in the students' smoking behaviors, these students created new roles for themselves that entailed actions of responsibility and ultimately contributed positively to the school and community.

Just as Follett perceived the importance of "fact-control" and the "reciprocal relating of all the factors in a situation" in the progress of an organization and in the success of leadership, Champlin and Mamary both worked continuously to align instructional practices with the mastery-learning discourse of the school district by using goals and "best knowledge" to drive and maintain the ecological health of the organization as a system.

In 1982 a statement entitled "Johnson City's Philosophical Principles and Practices" was published by Mamary and Champlin. It continues to align the rules and the strategies of the district to the present day.

Johnson City's Philosophical Principles and Practices

1. Almost all students are capable of achieving excellence in learning provided that students:

—Have sufficient time to learn

—Experience challenge with little threat

—Make decisions without fear of irreversible failure or criticism

—Have a supportive learning environment

—Have favorable learning conditions and quality instruction

—Have increased time on learning through active involvement in the learning process

—Have their performance expectations and be [*sic*] expected to achieve them

2. The instructional process can be changed to improve learning, provided that teachers:

— Improve planning procedures and clearly define expected outcomes and prerequisites

—Systematically control the learning process by teach ing the stated objectives and providing the help necessary to achieve them

—Systematically manage change so that improvement will be evolutionary and revolutionary

3. An essential function of schooling is to ensure that all students perform at high levels of learning and experience opportunities for individual success, provided that teachers:

—Reduce competition and encourage cooperation in learning

—Create a trust environment

—Understand that it is no longer appropriate for society to accept the fact that only 30% of the students now learn what is expected

—Eliminate the elitist notion of schooling

—Value all human beings

—Provide an affirming classroom

—Expect all students to learn and learn well

—Develop self-directed learning through opportunities and modeling

4. An effective instructional process varies the time for learning according to the needs of each student and the complexity of the task, provided that teachers believe:

—Learning is a continuous yet irregular process

—Aptitude is not defined as the ability to learn, but as the time necessary to learn

—Most students can learn what is expected, provided that they have the necessary time to learn

—The time to learn can vary

—The time necessary for students to learn a task need not be different, but [must be] appropriate

5. Success influences self-concept; self-concept influences learning and behavior, provided that teachers believe:

—The key to building a positive self-concept lies largely in what the teacher believes and communicates to his or her students

—When students come to view themselves as important, valued, and respected by their teachers and accept that they can learn, they will develop a healthy self-concept

—Students will build positive self-esteem when the classroom atmosphere is based on success rather than unnecessary failure

—Lack of success may make for a negative self-concept, alienate the student from the learning process, and foster negative behavior

—When schools provide successful learning experiences, students are more likely to develop positive self-concepts, which in turn facilitate learning and success

—Testing and reporting should be criterion-referenced, emphasizing individual growth and development the relationship of one individual to another

—A student's self-image is based upon his or her experiences in mastering certain tasks

—The more positive the self-concept the higher one's learning expectation and levels of performance

6. Staff and students share responsibility for successful learning outcomes when students and teachers believe:

—Learning is an active process requiring active participation of students and teachers

—Teachers should share the responsibility for learning by planning instruction carefully

—Students should share responsibility for learning by actively processing information to be learned and by interacting with the teacher, others in the class, and the instructional materials

—Students should also share responsibility for learning by preparing for homework assignments and examinations

7. Assessment of learning is continuous and directly determines instructional placement, provided that teachers believe:

—The appropriateness of the instruction can only be determined by continuous diagnosis of individual student skill attainment

—The diagnostic information resulting from the assessment enables them to prescribe the appropriate level of beginning instruction as well as determining when one skill has been mastered and instruction for the next skill should begin

—Assessment, feedback, and reporting should emphasize individual growth and development. It should
also be used to determine how well students have
learned what is expected, how well initial instruction
and the instructional process are working, and also as
a basis for determining necessary correctives

—Assessment should not be norm-referenced, but
rather should be self-referenced

—Students should be assigned to groups by demonstrated performance

8. Credit is awarded and recorded when learning is
assessed and validated, provided that teachers believe:

—Mastery learning varies the time necessary for
learning

—Credit is awarded when the material is mastered,
rather than at formal arbitrary periods during the
student's school career

—Students should be encouraged to continue to learn
by awarding them additional credit as they increase
their learning

—Grades can be altered to reflect new learning and
achievement[19]

Student achievement score data also continued to exert consid-
erable power in the alignment of beliefs and practices of staff within
the district. The validation of the achievement gains made by district
students in a study conducted by Vickery enabled the district to
receive a $75,000 renewable grant from the U.S. Office of Education in
1986, which was most recently renewed in 1994.[20] With this grant,
Johnson City became a member of the National Diffusion Network
with the purpose of disseminating nationally its program for comprehensive and systematic educational improvement. In the district's
preparation for the dissemination of their school improvement model,
Mamary and his staff articulated the Outcomes-Driven Developmental Model (see figure 1). Mamary and his staff also developed the
process of examining and identifying knowledge, beliefs, wants, and
actions in the district's "Success Connections." In the adoption of the
ODDM process, adopters arrive at responses to four "Success

Connection" questions that are extensive in scope, mutually compatible, and grounded in research literature. The following four questions are addressed:

1. What do we want?
2. What do we know?
3. What do we believe?
4. What do we do?

ODDM trainers assert that when a school district's staff and teachers are clear and consistent in their responses to these questions, they will find their goals, knowledge, beliefs, and actions produce a synergy that empowers everyone in the organization.[21] ODDM materials represent the synergy of the "Success Connections" in figure 4.

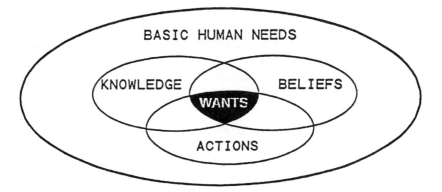

Fig. 4. The Synergy of Success Connections. Reprinted with permission from the Johnson City Central Schools, 1990.

Mamary's use of coactive power in the organization also manifested itself in the relationship of power with the teachers' association. The first contract to be negotiated under his superintendency was developed in meetings between the school board, administration, and faculty representatives without the assistance of a formal outside negotiator. This practice of informal negotiations had not occurred in the district since the 1960s, before the teachers had formally organized as the district's bargaining agent under the guidelines of New York's collective negotiations act. In this sense, Mamary's statement of "everybody in partnership" is strikingly reminiscent of George F.

Johnson's conception of the partnership of labor and management in the "Square Deal" and in his practices of building a cooperative commonwealth in the towns of Johnson City and Endicott. In both, the sphere of reciprocal influence Follett described resulted in a harmonious interaction between labor and management.

In Mamary's third principle—"everybody lives by the agreements until we change them"—an additional component of this coagency appears that Follett did not address. The consent of all members to live by the crafted agreement brings another dimension of meaning to coagency within a community. This consent implies a socially constructed contract on the part of the individual, and in this sense, entails a commitment to *live* by the agreement. Living by the agreement meant more than an agreement by the individual not to resist or get in the way of others carrying out the agreement; it meant an agreement to align, support, and cooperate in the fulfillment of this agreement. This principle procured a moral commitment by the individual to the action of the agreement. In this commitment, the individual acknowledged his or her responsibility to the common good or the "public" of the learning community in schools.

The knowledge/power of this publicly agreed-upon moral commitment to the integrated principle of any community—in this case, a learning community—is evident in the following incident. During a two day workshop held prior to the opening of the school year, the middle school principal was confronted by a teacher frustrated by the lack of cooperation of some of the teachers at the workshop. The teacher voiced her and her team's frustration,

> All along we have said that you don't have to cooperate with the program so long as you don't get in the way. That was appropriate for a long time, but now it isn't. If you are not cooperating, then you are getting in the way. There are people who are not cooperating and they are getting in the way of the rest of us. We are not going to name any names; you know who these people are. But we want you to do something about these people. That is your job. It isn't good enough any more to just stay out of the way. If they aren't cooperating, then they are in the way. We need their support and their active cooperation. If we don't have it, they are in the way.[22]

In this example of the internalization of the discourse, we observe the power of an integrated principle at work, for in this social contract, the agreement goes beyond one's responsibility to self to the overall responsibility to the group and by the group to the praxis of the contract. In this way, a discourse becomes an ethos wrapping the beliefs, the knowledge, the power, and the values of the group within the culture of these mutually held agreements.

This acknowledgment of an individual's responsibility for the whole school or community reveals the intentionality of the conduct of each member within the political context, capturing once again the meaning of praxis in leadership that Hodgkinson developed in his moral theory of leadership. In the relationship of coagency within the synergistic community of the Johnson City schools, this commitment to the common good worked to undergird and authenticate a universal agreement.

The students also became active agents and guardians of the social contract of Johnson City's instructional discourse and ethos. A teacher new to the school district had followed the district's instructional process as she understood it. She went through each of the prescribed steps and concluded the lesson with a test that she recorded in her grade book before beginning corrective instruction. However, several, not just one or two, began to protest loudly over her actions. They informed her the grades on a formative test were not recorded but serve as indication of who needs more instruction. The only recorded grade was the summative unit test.[23]

This "collective control" of the organization through a mutually binding social contract is rooted in the district's exploration of the meaning of responsibility in learning. In 1978, the central office and a small group of teachers in the middle school began to explore a process for the development of responsibility in the students at the middle school level.[24] Their investigation of "best knowledge" led them to the work of William Glasser and his process for the prevention of student failure in schools based in his practice of "reality therapy." Following the staff-development model of the district, a small group of teachers began implementing Glasser's philosophy on student needs and behavior in their classrooms. Their success in helping students take responsibility for their learning and for their behaviors in support of learning in school led to these teachers teaching others in the district.

In the next few years, Glasser's approach to student responsibility and learning became the accepted process of discipline within the district and also began to guide the overall conceptualization of human wants and needs in the district. As the numbers of staff and students using Glasser's approach to discipline and responsibility for self and others within their schools increased, four additional "desired student exit behaviors" were added to the existing academic outcome. These four outcomes are based in the learner's concept of self and responsibility, his or her relationship with others, and his or her use of process skills to learn independently and collaboratively. The five exit behaviors including the original academic outcome are:

1. Self-esteem as a learner and person
2. Academics—thinking and understanding
3. Self-directed as a learner and person
4. Concern for others
5. Process skills—problem solving—communication—decision making—accountability—group process

By 1986 when the "Success Connections" and the ODDM were formulated, Glasser's explanation of human needs became the "basic human needs" that interconnected with the "beliefs, wants, knowledge, and action" of the district in the ODDM system (see figure 4).[25] District staff also fully articulated student demonstration of the four additional exit behaviors on self-concept, responsibility, and collaboration in an extensive curriculum plan titled, "The Self-Directed Learner Dimension," which is a "continuum of learning experiences that accommodates all student in their progress in becoming self-directed learners."[26]

In this way, Glasser's reality therapy, renamed "control theory," shaped the knowledge and the language of Johnson City's discourse on power and responsibility. The internalization of the beliefs of control theory as well as those of mastery learning by the staff and students worked to align the actions of all in the district, and, in doing so, exercised power to control the beliefs and actions of the entire learning community.

In control theory, Glasser rejected the basic claims of the behavioral epistemology of stimulus-response theory, which postulated that human behavior is motivated by a stimulus outside of a person that causes him or her to respond or react. Glasser adamantly stated that "None of what we do is caused by any situation or person outside of ourselves."[27] Glasser maintained,

> All of our behavior, simple to complex, is our best attempt to control ourselves to satisfy our needs, but, of course, controlling ourselves is almost always related to our constant attempts to control what goes on around us.[28]

In this regard, every human behavior rises from within that person. One can only act, not react or respond. Essential to Glasser's theory is the belief that we *choose* every action we initiate. In his contention that each human in this sense is free and has control over each action, Glasser also insisted that "we always choose to do what is most satisfying to us at the time."[29] Within the context of schooling, Glasser applied the basic belief of control theory:

> If what is being taught does not satisfy the needs about which a student is currently most concerned, it will make little difference how brilliantly the teacher teaches—the student will not work to learn.[30]

Glasser continued by stating that there are five basic human needs built into the human genetic structure: "(1) to survive and reproduce, (2) to belong and love, (3) *to gain power* [italics are Glasser's], (4) to be free, and (5) to have fun." In explaining his italics for power, Glasser claimed the need for power is uniquely human and unlike the four other needs, which humans share to some extent with many other higher animals.[31]

"The need for power is particularly difficult to satisfy" in our culture, according to Glasser, because the mores of our culture "condemn those who openly strive for it, . . . [but] power itself is neither good nor bad."[32] Power permeates all relationships within society and culture as people strive to satisfy their own conception of how power is materialized in their lives through resources, benefits, or their perceptions of themselves. In the omnipresence of power even the "humble compete for who can be the humblest of all." Glasser claimed that the human need for power in schools cannot be subverted, will manifest itself negatively or positively in schools, and results in the tremendous failure of American schools. "Secondary schools have more losers than winners . . . because of the lack of access to power for students comes at just the time when students are beginning to experience the expressed need for power as part . . . of adolescence."[33]

In his examination of the meaning of these five basic human needs and their implications for schooling, Glasser established a comprehensive approach to schooling and behavior whereby teachers and school districts can help students satisfy these needs for the purpose of learning and establish the underlying belief that each person *chooses* his or her own actions, and therefore is responsible for this choice. In *The Quality School*, his subsequent work on the application of control theory to schools and on the management theory of W. Edwards Deming, Glasser posited three principles for the management of a school where power is shared.

1. Managing Without Coercion. This means that the principal must never coerce the teachers and the teachers must never coerce the students. It means eliminating all threats . . . to force a student or teacher to do what he or she does not want to do. . . . Both students and teachers must believe that a major goal of those who manage them is to treat them well.

2. Emphasizing Quality in All Assigned Academic Work. The teacher-manager's goal would be to persuade each student in every academic subject to do what the student would judge is quality . . . one of the requisites of quality is usefulness . . . students would never be held responsible for schoolwork that has no use in their lives.

3. Students Would Be Asked to Evaluate All of Their Work. In a quality school the evaluation of the work is done by both the student and the teacher with the emphasis on teaching the student how to do a good job of self-evaluation. The student is responsible for quality of his/her work.[34]

The knowledge/power of Glasser's control theory aligned closely with Mamary's conception and use of coactive power throughout his relationships in the school district. In this alignment, the discourse provided the language, rules, strategies, and concepts for understanding Mamary's management of the district and also exerted significant power to increase the unity and synergy that already existed in the schools. Control theory formed a synergistic pattern in harmony with the beliefs of mastery learning, for it maintained that power, like learning, is an unlimited resource and increases as it is shared. Power is not a force to be feared but to be channeled by each individual in the satisfaction of individual needs, and can increase learning.

In this paradigm, each individual has the power within to maximize learning in an environment where power is not coercive, but shared. This emphasis upon individual responsibility for self and conduct in regard to others and the overall community is dialectically, in Foucaultian terms, the ultimate form of power in the power/knowledge discourse, for it nurtures the individual's self-regulation for the purpose of learning and for the common good of the synergistic community. As an individual works with the basic belief that he or she chooses each action, his or her paradigm of reality is reconstructed; thereby, in the acceptance and embrace of this belief, each takes responsibility for each action conducted in the classroom and in the school. Again, in this praxis of schooling, events do not just happen; there is an intentional component to each behavior, a commitment within a sphere of consciousness where human values enter to inform each decision, and an ethic of responsibility emerges.

The shared, universal conception of power as coactive, as an unlimited, synergistic resource that worked to preserve the benefits and integrity of every individual and the ethic of purposeful social responsibility or social commitment to the agreement, as stated in Mamary's third principle, combined to create a cooperative commonwealth in the schools. The Johnson City schools under Mamary's leadership worked for this coactive process of schooling and community. Through this process, he and the others secured a public commitment to the quality of the social action of the whole community and formed Dewey's "invisible hand" of the public weal. This invisible hand bound them together and fused a moral identification with their commonly perceived interests, which led them to feel that they were greater than they knew.

9

Learning—Teaching—Leading

Language shapes consciousness, and the use of
language to shape consciousness is an important
branch of magic. . . . The magic that works is itself
a language, a language of action, images, of things
rather than abstracts . . . if we let the things themselves, in all the richness and complexity of their
existence, speak to us, we reverse the reversals, or
more—we dive below the cement-banked channels
of consciousness and reach the underground rivers
that are its source.
—Starhawk, Dreaming the Dark

As the culture of their school and
community slowly reshaped itself within a paradigm of synergy,
Johnson City faculty, staff, and students began to sense what Starhawk
has called the "power that comes from within." Returning to the root
meaning of the word "power," from the (late popular) Latin *podere*, she
gives voice to this meaning, "to be able," and calls this the power we
sense in a "seed, in the growth of a child, the power we feel writing,
weaving, working, creating, [and] making choices."[1]

This power, a basic human need according to Glasser, is the
power that constituted an authentic "we" in the questions the Johnson
City district calls the "Success Connections." In this chapter, we
explore the development and meaning of the follower in the "we" that
worked with and justified the leadership of Champlin and Mamary,
the "we" without which their efforts to reform schools from the top of
the organization would have been futile. This "we" in the human-to-
human work of schools is the wellspring of authentic power in changing humans and schools.

117

To find the source of the power of the "follower," of those who worked with the formal leaders of the district to create a paradigm for power in the district, we return to the first year of coactive power in Johnson City when Champlin began working with eight female teachers in the small elementary school of Oakdale. School minutes indicate that in the year before Champlin was hired these teachers had already been experimenting with team teaching and the concepts of student mastery and responsibility for their own learning.[2] Six elementary teachers involved in innovative programs traveled with school-board members and parents to Champlin's former district to observe the "open-structured" program this district was implementing under his guidance. These same teachers reported to the full board on the program in the spring of 1971 and recommended Champlin's hiring.

Champlin immediately began working with the full group of eight female teachers upon his arrival in Johnson City, and, as he said, began by rolling up his sleeves and working with them in a collaborative process of learning-teaching-leading to implement mastery learning in their classrooms. These teachers actively worked together in teams of three or two members as well as in the larger group of eight to implement this new form of learning on a daily basis.

In the summer immediately following this school year, Champlin recommended and received from the school board the funds to provide summer training in mastery learning for a new group of female teachers at the elementary level. In these summer training sessions, the eight original teachers worked with a wider circle of teachers to understand the language of mastery learning and to plan the implementation of mastery learning with the students in their own classrooms. During the following year, the teachers met and visited each other's classrooms to help each other implement the instructional reform.

In the years that followed, the process of teachers teaching teachers within the ecological context of their own classrooms and schools became the paradigm for staff development within the district and led to the formal adoption of this process by the school board in 1980. The concept, rule of language, and strategy of each innovative instructional process implemented in the district was nurtured and understood in a collaborative culture of learning where one teacher guided the learning of another teacher in the discourse of mastery learning and coactive power. The form of this staff development followed a cycle of learning-teaching-leading, a relationship where all three actions occur dynamically.

Vickery described the district's mastery model in staff development as "one where teachers learn and deploy [innovations] at their own rate"[3] with clear procedures for each step of the process. First, as learner, the teacher masters the research on the innovation; then he or she applies the practice in a controlled situation; next, the teacher begins to initiate the innovation in his or her own classroom, such as using a unit guide prepared by another teacher and with the coaching of that teacher; next, the teacher applies the practice without direct guidance, but with help available; and finally, if successful, the teacher designs new units based on the practice. According to Mamary, "Mistakes are not buried" when a new practice is tried "but are seen as opportunities for learning."[4]

At this stage, the teacher becomes a teacher of teachers. After demonstrating a sound knowledge of the theory behind the practice, this teacher will model the practice for others. Next, the teacher will become involved in the planning of unit guides to help others learn to apply the practice. These activities most often occur at the district's teacher center and teaching classroom. Finally, the teacher will coach the novice in the culture of his or her classroom and school. "All staff are encouraged to become experts in the instructional process . . . [and] become adept at explaining the program and helping others."[5]

During the last stage, teachers can become leaders in solving district problems; they are encouraged to become district spokespersons and can serve as consultants to other districts that want to learn about and perhaps adopt the Johnson City model of ODDM. At this stage, these teachers receive released time and any other resources needed from the district to enable them to function in their new roles.[6]

In this process of staff development, a culture of shared, innovative, good teaching grew. As essentially human communities of culture, where humans use language and tools to work in a social relationship, schools promote or inhibit good teaching and learning. In Johnson City the meaning of teacher expanded in this process to one of learner-teacher-leader. Learning-teaching-leading is a triadic, dynamic, interactive action occurring within one individual or with two or more individuals. The individual or individuals fluidly move through each of these three roles within the social-cultural relationship, sharing and creating the power of learning. The teacher-to-teacher process of learning-teaching-leading with one another in Johnson City's staff development process is a multidimensional, social interaction that can be interpreted as having philosophical, psychological, and ethical underpinnings in the Hegelian concept of mediation.

The Work of Language

The notion of mediation or *Vermittlung* constitutes one of the major concepts of Hegel's philosophical system. Hegel contended that a distinctly human type of activity depended on the transition from the immediate, animal type of satisfaction to the human satisfaction of a need removed from instinct.

> The being that acts to satisfy its own instincts, which—as such— are always natural, does not rise above Nature; it remains a natural being, an animal. But by acting to satisfy an instinct that is not my own, I am acting in relation to what is not—for me—intact. I am acting in a relation to an idea, a nonbiological end.[7]

The act of relating to an idea, to a nonbiological end, is the action of human mediation or, according to Hegel, the human activity of work. Hegel proposed that in the act of working, human consciousness is formed. It is "only by work, that man realizes himself objectively as a man. . . . In his work, he trans-forms things and trans-forms himself at the same time."[8] In this human capacity to mediate one's environment and oneself, the capacity to make meaning emerges and becomes a fundamental expression of the revolutionary activity of consciousness.

Directly and indirectly, the Hegelian concept of mediation influenced the thought and work of Lev Vygotsky (1896–1934), a postrevolutionary Soviet psychologist.[9] In his sociocultural theory of higher mental processes, Vygotsky applied Hegelian dialectical transformation to psychology.

Vygotsky extended the mediation in work through the use of tools in the natural and social world to the use of what he termed "signs," the symbolic actions of oral, physical, and written language, art, music, and number systems. Just as humans use tools to mediate their surroundings, humans use signs dialectically, internalize these culturally produced signs in the process, and dialectically, are themselves transformed. In their edition of Vygotsky's major psychological writings, *Mind in Society*, Cole et al. stated that "Vygotsky believed that the internalization of culturally produced sign systems brings about behavioral transformations and forms the bridge between early and later forms of individual development."[10] For Vygotsky, the symbolic making of meaning through signs in human activity was rooted in society and culture and was transformative, revolutionary, and essentially human. His work, therefore, strongly stressed the understanding of the use of sign in the culture or in the social relationship in which it occurred.

Vygotsky's theory of symbolic actions explains the first strength of the staff-development process of the Johnson City schools: the use of the symbols of the reform, the language of mastery learning in the cultural context of the classroom. The reform of Johnson City schools germinated in the social culture of the small elementary school where Champlin and eight teachers worked with their students and established strong ecological validity for these new practices. The language or the symbolic action of these ideas in shaping the powerful new discourse of mastery learning was worked out daily in the classrooms through the social and educational interaction of the teachers and learners. These teachers did not need to transfer their knowledge of mastery learning from a decontextualized setting such as an outside workshop or conference, thereby weakening the transfer of knowledge, but worked directly in the culture of their own classrooms.

This language-culture relationship allowed the teachers to construct their meanings of mastery learning directly with their own students. From a Vygotskian perspective, in the construction of meaning through symbolic action such as language, we embody and shape our cultural thought forms. In their use of "sign" in their sociocultural environment, the power in the act of naming a thought, in the use of language, is distributed. In the use of language, in the mediation of their environment and themselves, the teachers gained power and owned their thoughts and feelings.

Starhawk recognized this power in the naming and shaping of language. She stated that

> knowing something's name gives us power-with it . . . [and] the names we choose, the language that we use, also have power-with us, and shape use. Names . . . carry both the idea and the context.[11]

When the original group of female teachers and subsequent groups of primarily female teachers at the elementary level (whose identities are lost in the articulation of ODDM and the externally published documents of the district) began implementing the concepts of student mastery and individualized learning in their classrooms, they were continuously naming this action within themselves, with each other, and with their students and their parents. Through this language they transformed themselves and their students and distributed power. In the action of the triadic relationship of teaching, learning, and leading, a process in which at times the teacher leads the students but also responds to the needs of the student, and therefore is also led by the student, the action of power/knowledge lies. Here are the verbs of action that shape the names given to these actions in the discourse. The symbolic naming of the practice constructs the channel to convey meaning and to distribute the power.

Starhawk cautioned that when this naming becomes too separated from the ecological context of the actions or the verbs of the knowledge/power relationship, the possibility of estrangement exists. Defining estrangement as the removal of the human content and values in the relationships of work, Starhawk contended that this allows the "formations of power relationships in which human beings are exploited." She warned that

> whenever we choose the names that make things sound comfortable, acceptable, respectable, academically sound, scientific, we are almost always placing the thing we name back into the context of estrangement—removing its power and our own, alienating ourselves yet again.[12]

The distancing of language from the mediation of the work, the human activity that produced the power of the language, leads to educational estrangement. The ODDM code, like so many other models of educational reform, can become a form of estrangement too distant from the authentic "we" who work in schools when it is presented as a package that can be imprinted upon a school culture. Consultants who meet in hotel rooms and direct their presentations at those who sit at the top of the bureaucratic hierarchy of schools or at teachers who passively receive this alien knowledge are too far removed from the context of the social culture of the classroom of students. These models can cause educational estrangement and be exploitative in the sense that the good hopes for the school improvement held by those who attend these sessions are quickly subsumed upon reentry into their own cultures. Educational estrangement and alienation abound in the current dissemination of the language of education innovation, for it has lost its grounding and the power of working within the cultural context of the ideas and values of the triadic relationship. For this reason, many reforms are like brightly colored adhesive sheets applied to schools. They change the appearance of the surface but do not combine with the underlying actions and beliefs of the students, teachers, and administrators in schools and are unable to change school practices in a meaningful way.

Two additional important aspects are inherent in this process of staff development as a learner-teacher-leader relationship within the culture of the school: (1) the power of mediated learning for the construction of the meaning of the innovation or instructional practice, and (2) the support for a culture that values the act of caring for teachers as well as for students.

Both Vygotsky and, more recently, Feuerstein have conducted research on mediated learning, defined by Feuerstein as the "subtle, social interaction between the teacher and the learner in the enrichment of the student's learning experience"[13] and on its implications for the development and learning of children.

Feuerstein's research stems from the sociocultural roots of Vygotsky's work on mediated learning. Feuerstein built upon Vygotsky's emphasis that the mediated learning experience occurred in the interaction between a human being and his or her sociocultural environment. But Feuerstein has been most concerned with those experiences that influence the child's "propensity to learn," particularly the quality of those sociocultural interactions that help the learner to "become modified by exposure to stimuli in the direction of higher and more efficient levels of functioning and adaptation."[14] The mediator helps the learner "frame, filter, and schedule stimuli," states Feuerstein.[15]

Feuerstein says that three of the twelve major criteria in the mediated learning experience are universal to all mediated learning experience, and are therefore especially important for understanding the construction of language and meaning in the change of educational practice in the classroom. The three universal criteria of intentionality, transcendence, and the mediation of meaning form "the essence of what it is to be human."[16]

The first, the criterion of "mediation of intentionality and reciprocity," is that which changes an interactive situation from a random experience to an intentional situation. In the intentional experience, the mediating teacher alters the instructional role and is more than a mere provider of information. The teacher becomes a "source of constant affirmation that the objects or information involved are cognitively important to the learning, the capacity building of the student."[17] The reciprocity aspect of this criterion is the way the teacher underscores that it is the student's learning or cognitive processes that are really important, not the object or the information.

As reciprocity develops, "mediated learning becomes a two-way street."[18]

The second universal criterion is the mediation of transcendence in which the mediating teacher is not limited to that which originated the exchange with the learner but can widen the scope of interaction to goals that are beyond the independent cognitive level of the learner. "Transcendence ... assumes the constant enlargement of the learner's own need system and his/her dynamic, continuous change."[19]

The third universal criterion, the mediation of meaning, is important in the context of cultural transmission. This parameter is the "energetic dimension" of an interaction that generates the motivational, attitudinal, and value-oriented behaviors of an individual. In this universal the adult and the child exchange verbal interpretations of meaning with each other.

The ongoing staff development process of Johnson City included shared practice and mutual dialogue in each other's classrooms, weekly meetings, in-service sessions, in-district conference days, and summer training sessions. Led by district teachers, these meetings provided the opportunity for the mediated learning of novice teachers by experienced teachers whom they knew personally and whom they knew were successful in the implementation of the practice of mastery learning. Mediated learning in this process occurred at several interactive levels: the teacher working with the student during learning, the mediating teacher working with the novice teacher during learning and constructing meaning of the new instructional practice, and the dialectical action of the learner's and teacher's transformation in both relationships. Most importantly, in consideration of Feuerstein's research, the coaching of one teacher by another in the context of the classroom and in his or her own school district included these three criteria and propelled this learning to higher and more efficient levels of cognitive functioning and adaption.

In consideration of Feuerstein's first criterion, the Johnson City staff-development process included the intentionality of goal-driven, data-driven, shared practice and a locally developed language or discourse of mastery learning and control theory. The intentionality of this explicit alignment progressively channeled and narrowed the diversity of practices used by teachers. The second criterion, transcendence, was applied as the mediating teacher was able to modify and expand goals for different teachers. The mediating teacher knew these teachers and the culture of their classrooms and was able to help the novice teachers categorize and sort the concepts according to their own needs and the needs of the differing groups of children in their classrooms.

The third criterion, the mediation of meaning, was manifested as novice teachers were influenced by the values, attitudes, and the motivation of the more experienced, esteemed teacher. The mediating teacher became a validation of the practice's efficacy in increasing the student's achievement or performance and in improving teaching practices. This social valuing of the practice energized the interaction between the novice and mediating teacher and caused the novice to initiate the action.

Dialectically, as postulated in Hegelian and Vygotskian thought, the mediating teachers also were transformed as they worked with their own knowledge and with the knowledge and practices of the novice teachers and their students. Each of the mediating teachers sorted and categorized the language, concepts, and strategies of the new instructional practices collaboratively as they tried to implement these practices in their classroom, and met to reflect upon the results in conversation with the novice teachers. The district's psychological and financial support for these opportunities to engage in mediated learning of new instructional practices demonstrated that this aspect of the teachers' work was valued and rewarded. As a result, the teachers used the language of mastery learning and what they had learned through the mediation of each other's practice in their schools to engage continuously in a mediation process of their own learning and teaching.

District teachers also mediated the learning of their students through intentionality by explaining the purpose of the instructional process to their students. In district classrooms, teacher-made posters of the ODDM model are displayed on bulletin boards and explained to students at the beginning of each year. The teachers use the language of ODDM explicitly in their instruction. As the anecdote about the new teacher in the last chapter shows, the students within the district not only understood the ODDM instructional process as they participated in it through class after class, grade after grade, but were able to correct the missteps of the new teacher.

In their analysis of mediated learning and its implications for children's learning, Presseisen and Kozulin claim that Vygotsky's and Feuerstein's research on mediated learning supplants the behavioral model of learning with a new paradigm for education, in which mediation stresses the communal understanding of knowledge, not only in the collaborative sharing of experience but in the sorting and categorizing of ideas ... [and] assumes that instruction is more concerned with going beyond the information given, with the connecting the present with both the past and the anticipation of the future, than with mastering specific bits of here-and-now data.[20]

In this way, the process of mediated learning in the development of staff acted to support the district's movement from a paradigm based upon linear, discrete bits of knowledge to one of synergy. Mediated learning as a collaborative interactive force worked with the coactive conceptualizations of power found in Glasser's theory, replaced the behavioral paradigm, and increased the opportunities for the active construction of knowledge and for Mamary's conceptions of coactive power and leadership.

Similarly, the development process within the learning-teaching-leading cyclical relationship worked to strengthen the discourse of mastery learning in Johnson City as a systemwide cultural language, a phenomenon that has rarely emerged in other districts implementing Bloom's Learning for Mastery strategies. Much of the implementation of Bloom's Learning for Mastery strategies, as reported in the research of Block, Burns, Guskey, and others, has remained within a behavioral, quantitative orientation to the mastery-learning strategies. This perspective on learning grants the expanded potential of every student to learn under the right conditions, but views student learning tasks as sequential, discrete, segmented tasks of received knowledge controlled by the outside stimulus, the teacher.

The powerful, interactive dynamic of constructed knowledge and mediated learning is not released in this form of instruction, for the student is expected to conform to a sequential system of learning not necessarily responsive to the diversity of his or her needs as a learner. There is little opportunity for teacher or student mediation in the skill sequence or progression of the unit's steps, a critical factor in the integration of the discourse into one's thoughts and actions and in constructing one's own meaning of the knowledge and skills.

In many cases, these mastery-learning instructional programs have viewed the teacher as a technician who applies knowledge that has been externally validated outside of the ecological context of the teacher's classroom. Scientifically controlled, this instruction does not allow sufficient opportunity for a powerful discourse to generate.

Seeking to regulate teacher autonomy, such programs encountered passive teacher resistance or bold rejection. Although the mastery-learning literature has documented student achievement success, these isolated mastery-learning efforts have been, for the most part, effective in the content areas at the classroom or departmental level, but have fallen short of changing the overall instructional process at the grade or system level.[21]

The staff-development process as conceived in Johnson City created a culture of caring for teachers, learners, and all staff. As the Johnson City teachers worked collaboratively within their own contexts to change their instructional processes and to align with the educational discourse of the district, their collaborative work constructed a culture that placed a high value on human caring.

The reform of the instructional practice in the Johnson City schools was significantly female-dominated in that it began in the elementary schools, where the teaching population was over 95 percent female, moved into the middle school, where the number of female teachers outnumbered the male teachers by a substantial margin, and spread to the high school, where the male-female populations were roughly equal in the twenty-year period since its inception in 1971. This high proportion of female teachers is characteristic of American schools generally; nationwide 71 percent of the teaching profession is female.[22]

The first group of female teachers shared daily in smaller teams and weekly in a large team the instruction of the Oakdale building; they met regularly with Champlin to converse about their knowledge of and practices in their classrooms. They worked together closely to develop the discourse of a mastery learning that integrated the language of the research and embedded it in their knowledge and practice with their own students. They developed a means for instructional "real talk" as a way of connecting with others and acquiring and communicating new knowledge.

They then extended the power of their constructed knowledge to subsequent teams of the district's female teachers, who had received knowledge of the practice from Champlin and had begun to develop their own knowledge of mastery learning. Their mutual goals for the successful implementation of mastery learning in their classrooms to increase student achievement encouraged these elementary teachers to share their work and engage in mutual dialogue or "real talk" in collaborative relationships. In this way, they developed a coactive culture of trust and connection.

This opportunity for interrelationship outside the domain of their isolated classrooms also provided an affirmation of the ways in which women conceive power and responsibility. In a study of male and female fantasies of power, David McClelland found that "women are more concerned than men with both sides of an interdependent relationship," are "quicker to recognize their own interdependence," and equate power with giving and care.[23] Jean Baker Miller's analysis of male and female conceptions of power confirmed McClelland's research and revealed that "women stay with, build on, and develop in a context of attachment and affiliation with others," that "women's sense of self becomes very much organized around being able to make, and then to maintain, affiliations and relationship."[24]

In this research there is strong support for the importance of relationship and connection in a women's moral sense of self and in her construction of the ethical dimensions of her life. The collaborative relationship of the Johnson City teachers facilitated their common pursuit of a goal to increase their students' learning. Working together to help their students lent itself easily and naturally to this dimension of female psychology and conception of power. Their collaborative quest for the care of their students, in addition to the psychological and financial support of Champlin and Mamary, worked to supersede the conflicts and differences they may have had as individuals and engaged them in a process of creative integration for the cooperative solutions of problems related to their students.

Gilligan has argued that women perceive and construe social reality in terms of attachment, affiliation, and separation, and that those experiences which engage women in relationships of affiliation involve "women in a distinctive way." This distinctive way entwines women's sense of integrity into an ethic of care in which the "major transitions in women's lives . . . seem to involve changes in the understanding and activities of care."[25]

Noddings also claimed that a relational ethic, "an ethic of caring," differed dramatically from traditional ethics. Noddings stated that traditional ethics, such as that proposed by Kant, declare that "only those acts performed out of duty (in conformity to principle) should be labeled moral, [whereas] an ethic of caring prefers acts done out of love and natural inclination."[26] As a form of ethics, caring energizes both the giver and the receiver, according to Noddings, and is often "characterized in terms of responsibility and response."[27]

The fostering of an ethic of caring is also found in the district's student exit behaviors within the ODDM. The exit behavior, "concern for others," demonstrates the value the district places upon caring for staff and students. Vickery noted two student events as evidence of this outcome: (1) district students raised $15,000 through various fund-raisers to help build a senior citizens center in the community, (2) in a county Thanksgiving food drive for the needy, the students gathered more food than the eleven other school districts combined.[28]

The Johnson City staff-development process provided a strong means for the deep, systematic adoption of instructional reform. This process of mediated learning using the language of reform in the culture of the classroom and the school and of collaborative interaction for the caring of students, aligned with the discourse of mastery learning, established extensive networks of relationship and affiliation for the district's teachers. Over time, these teachers developed strong relationships of care, response, and responsibility for each other and for their students. This ethic of caring worked with the synergistic paradigm of mastery learning and coactive power to further the integrative principle of community in the schools. Together, staff mediation of both learning and human value contributed significantly to the feeling "that we are greater than we know."

10

The Work of Reforming Schools

Where is the Life we have lost in living?
Where is the wisdom we have lost in knowledge?
Where is the knowledge we have lost in informa-
tion?
　　　　　　—T. S. Eliot "Choruses from The Rock"

The cultural history of Johnson City, New York, from the community's beginning as a cooperative commonwealth in America's industrial age through the rise of its outcome-based schooling in the information age pioneered by corporations like IBM demonstrates both the promise and the reality of economic and educational synergy. The partnership of management and labor in Endicott Johnson's Square Deal, the IBM-dominated school board's push for a learning model that promised unlimited academic growth, and the praxis of leadership in the Johnson City schools are examples of relationships of coagency in which individuals and groups have found ways to satisfy human needs and to accomplish economic and educational achievement in a synergistic formula of human community. In the shaping and reshaping of this school-community culture, "individual self-interest was tempered by concern for social respectability and affection for community," allowing the common good to rise above self-interest. As it changed form over the past century in Johnson City, an integrated principle or ethos bound people together and fused a moral identification with commonly perceived and commonly held interests.

Just as the Endicott Johnson Corporation and its form of benevolent capitalism produced a high level of mutual economic benefit for both management and labor, and just as the IBM ethos introduced a high value for education in the community, so has the Johnson City school system and its form of outcome-based education, ODDM, produced a high level of educational benefits for all students. Whether the slogan is "90 percent of human beings are good" or "under the right conditions, all children can learn," the underlying principle is a vital belief in the unlimited capacity of the human being to work, to learn, and to do good.

In this final chapter, I examine the sustainability of the ODDM model in Johnson City and its dissemination to other school districts and states, and conclude by exploring the meaning of human action and synergy in schools and communities.

Sustaining ODDM

As the only total school curriculum model validated by the National Diffusion Network,[1] the Johnson City schools entered their third decade of systemic transformation in 1992. With the retirement of Albert Mamary in 1993, Lawrence Rowe, who started teaching in the district in the mid-1970s and later progressed to principal and assistant superintendent, became the district's third superintendent since 1971. Having worked actively in the development of the reforms and with ODDM, Rowe is currently committed to this paradigm of synergistic schooling.

This method of "growing one's own" leaders and of hiring from within the system has been characteristic of the personnel decisions made within the district. Prospective teachers often begin as substitutes who are initiated into the district's model through mediated learning, and if successful in adapting to the practices of the districts are hired to fill a teaching vacancy. These new teachers also participate in peer coaching in the weeks before their first permanent year of teaching. This orientation and ongoing mediated learning ensure that a new teacher becomes acculturated into the dominant discourse of the district. The learner-teacher-leader cycle of staff development also continues to encourage staff to aspire to different levels within the system.

In the past five years, systemic interconnection of the district's discourse on ODDM and coactive power has extended to special populations of students who are either academically or behaviorially challenged or both. With parental agreement, the district staff has been incorporating mildly to severely disabled students into the regular classroom. An on-site alternative secondary school is available for students who are having recurring behavioral difficulties in regular classrooms. Continued interaction with regular school activities is maintained for the student while individualized instruction and counseling are arranged until the student can return, when possible, to regular schooling.

Having abandoned I.Q. testing in the late 1970s, the district requires all students, beginning in the third grade, to complete one independent research investigation yearly. Accelerated learners are district-identified or self-identified through recommendation and evidence of student achievement and effort. These learners are heterogeneously grouped in classrooms, but may engage in several independent research investigations each year.

The data-driven alignment of the district initiated under John Champlin has continued through measurements of student achievement, attendance, retention, extracurricular participation and volunteer activity, and postsecondary enrollment. Since 1984 the percentage of students in grades 1–8 who have performed at or above grade level on standardized tests has ranged from 80 to 90 percent. Beginning in the 1991–92 school year, all ninth-grade students have been enrolled in first-year algebra and work to mastery in the time-flexible completion of this course. Since the early 1980s, the student dropout rate has remained below 5 percent.[2]

Since 1986 the percentage of Johnson City students receiving the rigorous New York Regents diploma have exceeded both county and state averages. Almost 75 percent of the district's students earn the Regent's diploma, up from about 60 percent in 1978. This percentage is almost 15 percentage points higher than one of the upper-middle-class districts in Broome County and comparable to that of two other districts with higher levels of socioeconomic status.

As reported by Vickery, Johnson City has also more than doubled the percentage of its graduates who win Regents scholarships. These scholarships are awarded to graduates based upon their scores on college admissions tests and operate on a zero-sum basis in each county in New York. "Thus the graduates of a district may improve and score higher on college admission examinations but only if their improvement is greater than the improvement of the graduates in the rest of the county, can they increase the number of Regents scholarships they receive."[3]

Amid these continuing patterns of high achievement for a very large percentage of students in the district is one interesting academic indicator that suggests the continuing legacies of both Endicott Johnson and IBM, as well as the effect of the socioeconomic status of the community overall. Although the district has more than doubled the percentage of students who win Regents scholarships, the number of students taking college admissions tests has only increased 5 percent in the past ten years. As reported by Vickery, data on the Regents scholarships combined with data on the Regents diplomas indicates that Johnson City has furthered the educational opportunities for that portion of the student population that usually would not have the credentials to go to college. The district has helped these students obtain the achievement and credentials to attend college, but has not been able to increase dramatically the number of those who do.[4] Vickery's data also reported that those Johnson City students who are pursuing postsecondary education are going to four-year colleges, instead of two-year colleges as they had a decade ago, and that more of these students are attending higher-status four-year colleges than Johnson City graduates had done in the 1970s.

While the district has managed to increase the number attending postsecondary institutions, it is a small number compared to those who are prepared to do so. This small improvement in college enrollment is a reflection of the continuing lower socioeconomic status of this community as compared to surrounding communities. It also indicates an ongoing cultural and economic resistance to the value of postsecondary education that is neither compulsory nor subsidized by public taxes.

The lingering social ethos of both Endicott Johnson and IBM is revealed in this data. Those who do attend college appear to aspire to a higher level within the social "elect" and value this education strongly—a reflection of the IBM ethos. But the majority of the population are content to continue EJ's legacy by viewing the high school diploma as the terminal degree. The significant change is that those students who hold this degree graduate with a higher level of achievemen than the former EJ children, who were placed in lower-track programs and did not receive sufficient credentials for college entrance. The district has provided the opportunity for college, but many do not choose to take it.

In many respects, the demographics of Johnson City today are similar to those of 1970. The population has stabilized at approximately seventeen thousand. The majority of its residents are still primarily of East European descent, although the community has seen a substantial percentage increase in the number of Asian and Hispanic residents each year. This population has more than tripled in size. Surrounding communities are still wealthier; 10.5 percent of Johnson City residents are classified by the 1990 Census as living in poverty. Per capita income is $12,497 and the median income for a household is $24,297. Approximately 22 percent of the population is over sixty-five years of age, still considerably higher than the national figure of nearly 13 percent.[5] The median price of a house is $68,900, a substantial increase from 1970, reflecting the national inflation of home prices as well as the increased desirability of owning a home in the community. However, housing in the center of town is still relatively cheap. Relatively few people are employed in the shoe industry, most workers having moved to jobs in small business, retail, and service industries, and in the high-technology firms in the area.[6]

Acclaim resulting from local, state, and national awards and publications has worked to change the image of the school district and, to some extent, the community in the area. Through the 1970s, Johnson City was perceived as a blue-collar shoe community with a "greaser school district" and was avoided by county realtors and middle-class home buyers. Since the mid-1980s, however, prospective buyers have sought to purchase homes in the outer suburban and rural areas of the district and, if unable to do so, have requested to pay tuition for their children to attend the schools.

One can conclude that outcome-based education in Johnson City has substantially increased the academic achievement and educational opportunities for its students and has changed the dominant paradigm within the school culture. However, at this time in the history of the community, the increased value for education and increased student benefits within the school culture have not greatly budged the scarcity paradigm of the outer cultural ground and community. This may possibly change when those students who have completed twelve years in the Johnson City district return to the community, get jobs, and raise families.

Disseminating ODDM and OBE

As recognition of the district's educational accomplishments increased, administrative staff and district teachers began to conduct training in the district's model of outcome-based education for other school districts in 1980. The district also opened its annual conference to other educators in the early 1980s to answer innumerable requests for information on the district's programs and to accommodate educators' requests to visit its classrooms. With the validation of the Outcomes Driven Developmental Model (ODDM), the process of dissemination became formalized through a prescribed adoption procedure. As of 1994, over seventy school districts in twenty states had adopted ODDM.

The adoption procedure for ODDM entails twenty-three days of training for the adopting district's staff over a two-year period. A leadership team comprised of building principals, a central-office instructional leader, teachers from each building, and school-board members visits Johnson City initially for one day and then is trained by Johnson City staff and other consultants at the adopting district's site. During the two years of training, the adopting district establishes and initiates twenty components of ODDM, including such areas as the research base, mission, student outcomes, a staff-development model, a management model, curriculum organization, instructional process, and classroom practices.[7]

The minimum criteria for adoption are as follows:

> Establish all twenty components of ODDM. ODDM is performance-based rather than time-based. While many, if not most, adopters require two years of training and implementation to function at the self-direction stage, some adopters may be able to design and implement the twenty components in a shorter period of time due to a more advanced state of readiness.[8]

During the two-year adoption process, the leadership team will design a comprehensive system of educational reform for virtually every facet of the district's organization. The brevity of this period of adoption and implementation contrasts remarkably with the twenty-year evolution of ODDM in Johnson City, its slow percolation through the elementary and secondary levels, and its gradual articulation and implementation by every staff member during two decades. Immediately one wonders, in such a rapid imprint of an externally applied model, how can an authentic "we" be created? How is it possible for each teacher to engage in a mediated learning process with an experienced teacher who has worked through the instructional process and curriculum with his or her students and is ready to teach and learn with a novice teacher? How is it possible for the adopting district's staff to construct a language and action plan for school improvement whose meaning is thoroughly worked through and understood in the culture of the district involved? How can the mastery outcomes and coactive power discourse integral to the transformation of the district from a paradigm of scarcity to synergy develop in such a short time?

Such a swift transmission of the ODDM process contradicts the heart of the praxis that fueled the reform of the Johnson City schools. These troubling questions challenge the authenticity of the adoption process and create doubt regarding the depth of these applications of educational reform.

Nonetheless, the adoption of ODDM and OBE by local school districts spread to over forty states, like an outbreak of influenza, in the past decade. OBE has even crossed national borders and is being disseminated in Western Europe and Australia. Relentless public pressure on American schools has fueled an astonishing demand for information and training on OBE, leading to the creation of several consortia of consultants in the process and lucrative contracts for their services.

Two major camps of OBE consultants with differing philosophical orientations to educational reform emerged in the 1990s. The divergence of philosophies developed over the extent to which students will demonstrate what they know and can do, the generic definition of "outcomes." Originally, nearly all OBE proponents focused upon student academic outcomes in schooling. Arguing that outcome-based education should extend to life goals, a group led by William Spady formed the High Success Network to develop a model for school improvement that focused upon those academic and personal outcomes students needed in preparation for lifelong learning and their future roles as adults.

Spady, whose roots lie in the competency-based educational movement of the late 1970s, defines his model of outcome-based education as a transformational approach. This model treats "subject-matter as 'enabling outcomes' related to the 'performance roles' students will play in the future." In his hierarchical model termed the "Demonstration Mountain," students move through levels of content skills and higher-order competencies to operate within "authentic life contexts . . . to demonstrate what real people do to be successful *on a continuing basis* in their career, family, and community."[9] At the highest level in this model, there is a strong emphasis on critical thinking and problem solving by students and a strong demand for ownership, self-direction, and self-assessment.

The original proponents of OBE have continued their focus on ODDM, and have recently developed a new, more formalized partnership, "Partners for Quality Learning." This group consists of loosely coordinated members of the Network of Outcome-Based Schools minus Spady and his Demonstration Mountain proponents. This new partnership includes practitioners such as Champlin, Mamary, and others at the National Center for Outcome-Based Education whose work has been published in their journal, *Quality Outcomes-Driven Education*, and university academics such as James Block, Robert Burns and others who have widely published their research on mastery learning and outcomes in external publications and in their own journal, *Outcomes*.[10]

However, as school districts have rushed to implement some form of OBE, the research on student performance in these adopting districts has been "largely perceptual, anecdotal, and small scale," according to Evans and King.[11] In their search for hard data on the effects of OBE upon student achievement, King and Evans found the strongest evidence for substantive success in the Johnson City schools and in those districts that have adopted ODDM. Their evidence was based mainly on data released by Johnson City on their own schools, data from Minnesota and Missouri, and an evaluation report on the thirty-four districts in Utah that had adopted ODDM, the highest number of districts in any state.

The Utah evaluation data consisted of interviews, questionnaires, and student achievement performances and made the following conclusions:

—Implementation of OBE generally requires a restructuring of the entire educational system and consequently takes a significant period of time.

—More OBE implementation takes place in districts that have adopted ODDM as a model than in other districts.

—More OBE implementation takes place in elementary schools than in secondary schools, and in smaller districts than in larger districts.

—Although the evidence is limited, districts with more complete implementation of OBE also appear to demonstrate higher student achievement gains.

—Districts using ODDM seem to be experiencing the most successful implementations.[12]

From their review of OBE and mastery-learning literature and data, Evans and King uncovered three themes on the restructuring efforts of OBE: (1) mastery learning and its ODDM implementations have been effective at the classroom and building levels, (2) ODDM can work and is readily adapted into traditional systems, and (3) OBE appears to benefit low-achieving students while having questionable effects on high-achieving students. They concluded that the adoption of OBE models such as ODDM had significant potential to effect change within traditional systems of education, but that its ability to transform school districts remained to be seen. They also were convinced that "traditional studies are not rich enough to portray the changes that an OBE system may inspire" and called for "innovative evaluation methodologies that truly capture the excitement of real and lasting change in schools."[13]

Aside from the mass of educators who have overwhelmingly embraced OBE reforms, the public response has been vocal and mixed. Many citizens, relying upon the judgments of local, state, and national educational experts and outside consultants, have supported their school boards' decisions to approve the adoption of outcome-based education in their schools. However, citizens in Pennsylvania, Connecticut, Missouri, Virginia, Arkansas, and several other states have rallied against OBE, and in some cases have succeeded in quashing any prospect of its adoption.

In October 1993, Virginia's governor halted the state board of education's initiative toward an outcome-based education plan. The board's president declared the proposed OBE program "dead" as a result of "widespread misunderstanding. . . . The program was designed to set standards for the skills and abilities students were expected to acquire by age 16."[14] Critics claimed the standards elevated instruction in values and self-esteem over academics, while supporters defended the program but stated that it had not been explained clearly to the public.

Similar attacks on OBE have occurred in nearly all states where the state government has tried to adopt OBE as a mandate for its local districts. In their push for OBE programs, various state governments have used the model as a means of strengthening their hold on local education. In a century of increasing state control of education, many states, such as New York, have had curriculum goals and objectives for their students or, like Texas for several decades, mandatory textbook adoptions. However, in the 1980s after the release of *A Nation At Risk* almost every state tightened its monitoring of local districts through required testing programs for students and teachers or increased graduation requirements. Nonetheless, local districts could still determine how they would meet their state's curriculum goals or how they would teach the knowledge and skills assessed in state tests or in courses required by the state. With states' efforts to regulate both academic and affective outcomes through OBE, they took a bolder step toward the control of curriculum.

As the Virginian supporters of OBE have claimed, information on OBE has often been poorly stated, vague, and steeped in jargon and, therefore, easily misunderstood or misinterpreted by opponents already mistrustful of government. But the strongest public attacks have focused upon two aspects of the reform and have united two groups of citizens who generally hold opposite political views: conservatives, often religious fundamentalists, who fear OBE because they believe it will cause "mind-control and meddling in family values," and suburban, more liberal citizens who fear that it will cause academic mediocrity in public schooling.[15] Both groups have used each other's fears, arguments, and research in their opposition to OBE.

Conservative opposition has issued from such groups as the Eagle Forum, the Focus on the Family, the fundamentalist Christian Coalition, and Citizens for Excellence in Education (CEE). The last group is a "grassroots ministry dedicated to restoring Christian values in the public schools."[16] Founded in 1983 by Robert Simonds, the CEE has had an agenda advocating prayer in school, school choice, and school programs emphasizing Christian values, patriotism, and capitalism. The list of programs they oppose runs much longer and includes drug education; sex education; multiculturalism; reading materials that include fantasy and the portrayal of satanic roles such as those of witches; self-esteem education; critical thinking skills; cooperative learning; global education; and most recently, outcome-based education. In 1985, Simonds published a booklet titled "How to Elect Christians to Public Office," which urged Christians to run for school-board elections and began an intensive effort to develop local chapters of CEE throughout the United States. By 1991 Simonds claimed that CEE had helped to elect 1,257 school-board members nationwide and held high hopes for each upcoming election.[17]

In Pennsylvania, Peg Luksik, a former pro-life crusader, special-education teacher, and mother of five children, became a leader in CEE and began to organize citizen opposition to outcome-based education when the state first proposed the reforms in 1991. Luksik, her colleagues in CEE, and a subgroup called the Pennsylvania Coalition for Academic Excellence blanketed local districts with information to parents that condemned Pennsylvania's proposal for OBE. A chapter newsletter declared, the secular education community has chosen Pennsylvania as the test state for the American version of the New World Order. . . . Humanist doctrine has been written into the Pennsylvania State School Code: Self Esteem, Self Worth, Wellness and Fitness, Adaptability to Change, Higher Order Thought, Learning Independently, Ethical Judgement, Appreciating and Understanding Others, the State supplanting the family, and all without discrimination of sexual orientation. . . . The big guns of Outcome Based Education (OBE) have made their appearances. . . . This is where the battleground lies for the future of all students in the 21st century. We sit on the cutting edge of the New World Order, and believe me, the view is not pretty.[18]

Declaring a holy war on OBE, local members of CEE descended on the state capitol and local school-board meetings, arguing fervently and incessantly against the proposed state-reform proposal. They besieged state legislators with letters and phone calls, demanding to know why the state-curriculum guidelines were designed to mandate the teaching of explicit personal values such as "appreciating and understanding others," a "tolerance of differences," and "respect for diversity." They interpreted these outcomes as appreciation, tolerance, and respect for homosexuals and for lifestyles considered "abhorrent" to Christian fundamentalists. They wanted to know why the state was trying to destroy the traditional Christian family.

Their investigations of the High Success Network, ODDM, and the educational literature on OBE also revealed its emphasis on students' critical thinking, independent problem solving, self-responsibility, and independence or self-direction. Many Christian fundamentalists and conservatives view this emphasis on independent, individualistic thinking, minimally, as an encroachment upon the domain of the family, or, maximally, as a plot to undermine the family structure in order to establish a state religion of secular humanism.[19]

In its simplest definition, secular humanism comprises a set of ethical standards that primarily emphasizes a person's ability to interpret and guide his or her own moral actions rather than relying on God. Glasser's control theory, four of ODDM's desired student exit behaviors and Spady's "complex unstructured task performances" focus on the development of self-direction, personal ownership, and self-assessment of moral action—all outcomes that challenge the basic tenet of Christian fundamentalists who unilaterally believe that the sole source of ethical and moral authority is God and the Bible.[20]

Christian fundamentalist groups are concerned about the emphasis on the demonstration of student outcomes through the explicit learning of value outcomes and critical-thinking skills, for they are cognizant of the effectiveness of mastery learning in producing student academic outcomes. Although they have publicly questioned data on its ability to increase student achievement, labeling it a smokescreen used to gain support from more moderate parents, fundamentalist educators in private church schools and in home schooling use curricula and workbooks based on the principles of mastery learning.[21]

Their relentless campaign attracted increasing numbers of people throughout the state, stunned many state legislators with its ferocity, and found an ally in another pro-life crusader, Governor Robert Casey. Casey threatened to stop the whole educational package unless the outcomes the CEE found objectionable were removed or modified to his approval. After several months of wrangling, several outcomes were dropped or removed and the plan received Casey's approval. By May 1993 the plan had proceeded through both houses of the legislature and a regulatory commission, but by that time the changes were not enough for Luksik and the CEE, who were still opposed to the plan. They raised such a ruckus that several legislators threatened to pass a resolution to block the curriculum regulations, but they were unable to gather sufficient numbers to squelch the reform.[22] After her efforts in Pennsylvania, Luksik traveled to several other states to help their local CEE chapters; she returned to mount an ill-fated gubernatorial bid in 1994 in Pennsylvania. At the time of this writing, the incoming Republican governor has declared the regulations voluntary for local districts.

Critics in middle-class suburbs with more moderate to liberal political leanings believe state directives implementing OBE "would disturb and drag down their schools . . . to solve . . . the failure of schools in cities . . . overwhelmed by large numbers of poor children."[23] The collapse of Connecticut's plan for school reform and the creation of academic outcomes for grade levels K–12 is an example of the power of this group of citizens.

Led by Kay Wall, a former businesswoman in upscale Greenwich and president of a local parent/teacher organization, citizens organized chapters of a group calling itself the Committee to Save Our Schools (SOS) in one-third of the state's school districts.[24] At grassroots meetings and on radio talk shows, Wall and her supporters ripped apart the state's Commission on Educational Excellence plan to design a "world-class educational system" that in theory would establish rigorous standards for what students should know and be able to do.

The commission's charge from the state was broad in that it was asked to consider a wide range of issues, including family services, preschool education, classroom technology, the school calendar, teacher training, and tenure.[25] Of the forty-three members comprising the commission, two were teacher representatives appointed by Connecticut's two major teacher unions and only one represented parents. This lack of representation, the commission's recommended changes in teacher tenure, and its support for experimental charter schools angered the unions and caused them to oppose the plan. They joined Wall's group in the massive public relations campaign against the reform.

Wall and SOS attacked the plan for student academic standards and labeled it outcome-based education, declaring that OBE would limit teaching to the level of the slowest learners by eliminating grades and forcing homogeneity among students. Wall reportedly denounced OBE as "a kind of egalitarianism that winds up forcing equality of results, rather than equality of opportunity, and we, frankly, consider that un-American."[26] However, the group caused the greatest controversy over their allegations that OBE taught values and challenged the rights and foundation of the traditional family—the same fears raised by Luksik's group in Pennsylvania, Simond's CEE, and other Christian conservative spokespeople and organizations.

Denying any alliance with the Christian Right, Wall stated her opposition was based primarily upon OBE's threat to academic rigor and expectations. Her group's opposition had originated in some of Connecticut's wealthiest suburbs, where 75 percent of the parents were satisfied with the state's current education. These parents feared the plan's challenge to existing schooling, in which their children had been well served, scored high on SATs, and as a result attended good colleges. Aware of OBE's underlying mission to increase educational benefits for all children, these citizens were the parents of the "winners," the children who fared well in school and benefited from a larger share of current educational resources. Viewing education as a competitive, zero-sum game, they feared OBE would close the achievement gap by holding all students to the pace of the slowest students by "dumbing down the curriculum" and leaving their children with less.

The relentless campaign of SOS drew in economically privileged parents and religiously conservative parents as well as middle-of-the-road parents who were distrustful of the vague terminology of the plan and state government. Addition of the force of the state's teacher unions to this strong base of public opposition doomed any passage of the state plan.

How successful will these forces of opposition to OBE be in other states? Although they were not able to defeat Pennsylvania's adoption of state curriculum outcomes as they had in Connecticut, they did force the removal of many of the value outcomes they viewed as objectionable. They also have been able to instill fear in the hearts of local superintendents through the election of increasing numbers of like-minded citizens to their school boards. Their political opposition in Pennsylvania, Connecticut, and in other states has seriously tainted OBE's name as a reform movement.

But in light of the historically grim fate of education-reform movements in the United States, the deeply entrenched structure of the existing American system of education, and educational policy-makers' penchant for quick fixes in their dissemination and replication of OBE, these groups may have little reason to fear OBE. They do not realize that American educational leaders, in their bandwagon approach to reform and their rapid application of the latest program, not only underestimate the power of the local constituency but also neglect the underlying local culture of schools where the thoughts, language, and actions of the daily work of schools and communities are embedded and where the power to change schools lies.

Synergistic Reform

The development of synergistic reform in the schooling of Johnson City provides a rich portrait of the praxis of ethical conduct in a political context, and illustrates this process in the transformation of an American school. The process of synergistic reform occurs in the mediation of humans through work and ethical relationship in the culture of schooling.

To reproduce the transformation that occurred in Johnson City in other American schools, educational leaders at the local, state, and national levels must rethink their own ways of knowing about learners, teachers, and schools. The notion of a magic bullet, of a miracle model going into the bloodstream of American schools and quickly fixing the system, is faulty. The reform of the Johnson City schools teaches us that even a whole systems approach such as ODDM does not work through a superimposed application and will not percolate through the system in the short period of two or even five years, the average length of employment for a superintendent in U.S. school districts. The more than twenty-year succession of superintendents in Johnson City provided a sustained official commitment to this model and developed a praxis of leadership in the daily context of the school culture that valued all people in the organization. A paradigm shift from scarcity to synergy, the praxis of the leader and the led, and the reshaping of the school culture are holistic, time-consuming approaches to curing schools. These types of change cannot be a top-down reform; those wishing change must work with the local community of the individual school district.

In rethinking their ways of knowing, leaders who want to reform schools also need to free themselves from Newtonian and Weberian conceptual frameworks in their analysis and explanation of schooling. The Newtonian perspective holds that human behavior in schools can be understood through a linear, sequential linkage of one unit of analysis to the next. Unit analyses of schools primarily focus upon one aspect of the system such as the principal, the curriculum, the structure, the teacher, the pedagogy, or the learner. The isolation of this unit from the culture of schooling may be necessary for research in the laboratory, but by its very nature it is estranged and static. Therefore, when the unit is reintroduced without alignment with every other part of system, the surrounding culture absorbs, changes, or rejects the improved unit.

Similarly, a Weberian conception of organization as a hierarchy interacting through channels of communication is limiting and unresponsive to complex environments. Pyramids are structurally sound and efficient when the goals of the organization are simple and one-dimensional, as in the manufacture of a product or the accomplishment of well-defined tasks, but the form is unresponsive to the complex, chaotic demands of the changing, interactive culture of late-twentieth-century America and to the multiplicity of needs of American students. The self-contained, self-supporting pyramid is too easily removed from the context and values of the surrounding culture, too isolated from nature and from the interaction of the lives of human beings outside the pyramid.

First, the development of a dynamic, creative, systemic integration of educational reform into the culture of American schools will entail an understanding of the interactive totality of the deep culture of schooling. The social, economic, political, historical, and institutional culture of school and community will need to be respected before it can be reshaped. Those who seek to change the local school district need to move from one cultural dimension to another without losing sight of the totality of the culture of the local school and the community.

Second, those who initiate change in schools need to understand the mediated action of human work within human culture. This mediated action is the daily work of every human within the system of schools. As we labor alone or together, with tools and with language, each of us constructs the meaning of our work and, dialectically, of ourselves. This meaning affects our lives and seeps into our thoughts, our language, our choices, our beliefs, and our sense of ourselves. In our work, we find the possibilities of life, and invent for ourselves and our children how we will behave and who we will be in our societal roles. Even in our choosing not to take action, we work and are transformed.

Our work is a "daily death" according to Simone Weil,[27] a measure of life whereby each of us turns body and soul into the means for survival and reproduction, love and belonging, power, fun, and freedom. In working, we become essentially human as we separate ourselves from other biological creatures and, in Weil's eyes, journey to our death. But, in this "daily death," in our work, we dialectically recreate or transform ourselves through the mediation of action and of language to construct that meaning of the self that each of us holds of consciousness, of our spirit.

In the daily work of the leader, teacher, and learner and the learner-teacher-leader, the power/knowledge discourse of mastery learning and coactive power is actualized. Through the language and tools of this discourse, each human in Johnson City worked to increase the learning and power of all students and through this daily work, they, too, were transformed. Those who wish to change schools need to recognize the importance of person-to-person mediation through tool and language, and construct the means to support such mediation.

This daily work in deep culture also formed the foundation of George F. Johnson's cooperative commonwealth and his partnership of labor and management. Johnson worked through tools and language to create a discourse of the Square Deal in many ways, e.g., by working directly with his factory workers; by the continuous publishing of his own writings, and those of his workers, on the power of the Endicott Johnson system; by tying the welfare of the corporation to the welfare of the workers through the sinews of such services as health care, mortgages, pensions, cafeterias, and recreational facilities; and by embedding management in the culture of the workers by requiring his managers to work their way through the factories and to live in the factory communities.

The second generation of Johnsons did not fully sustain this work of mediated action and language in the shaping of the EJ discourse. In exchange for workers' loyalty and refusal to unionize and in compensation for their lower hourly wages, they continued some of the company's services, but they began to distance themselves from the work of their factories in the 1950s. In response to foreign competition, they moved their plants to other states and Puerto Rico, away from the communities of Johnson City and Endicott. As the third generation distanced itself even farther from the content and values of EJ's work and culture, they were unable to prevent the economic disintegration of the corporation.

The mediated action of the work of the leaders, teachers, and learners of the staff, students, and community in the culture of the Johnson City school-community will ultimately determine the future sustainability of ODDM in the district. Only if they are able to sustain their work of the power/knowledge discourse of ODDM through active language and meaningful action will they prevent an estrangement from this power.

Finally, the ethical action of caring and commitment will need to infuse the daily work of those within the culture of the school-community. A praxis of synergy relies upon the creation and integration of an authentic sense of "we," of trust, and of a genuinely shared power in schooling that includes students. Ethical action involves a conscious commitment to moral action and language, a commitment that is shaped through the building of coactive relationship with others over time. Formal leaders who try to imprint models of reform upon their schools and then move quickly onto the next school district do not provide the power for the creative integration of humans nor for synergy. The bonding of community for the common good of all in the formation of an ethos comes only through the active, long-term investment of self by both those leading and following. Such action occurs at eye level within the local school culture and community with people who have some sense of their community, and is resistant to state mandates.

To reform schools, to find the Life lost living in schools bound by scarcity, to find wisdom in the overabundance of knowledge about schools, we will need to gain ways of knowing that are centered in the mediation of daily work, shared power, mutual dialogue, and ethical relationship, and are embedded in the culture of the school-community.

Notes

PREFACE

1. Michael W. Apple, *Education and Power* (Boston: Routledge & Kegan Paul, 1982). Henry A. Giroux, *Ideology, Culture, and the Process of Schooling* (Philadelphia: Temple University Press, 1981). Henry A. Giroux, *Schooling and the Struggle for Public Life: Critical Pedagogy in the Modern Age* (Minneapolis: University of Minnesota Press, 1988).

2. Martin Carnoy and Henry M. Levin, *School and Work in the Democratic State* (Stanford, California: Stanford University Press, 1985), 24.

3. Robert N. Bellah, Richard Madsen, William M. Sullivan, Ann Swidler, and Steven M. Tipton, *Habits of the Heart: Individualism and Commitment in American Life* (New York: Harper & Row, 1985).

4. Ibid., 287–88.

5. Cheryl T. Desmond, "An Historical Analysis of the Dynamics of School and Community Reform" (Ph.D. diss., Syracuse University, 1990).

6. John Lukacs, *Historical Consciousness or The Remembered Past* (New York: Schocken Books, 1985), 32.

7. Ibid., 33–35.

8. Ibid., 35.

9. Ibid., 34.

10. Burton R. Clark, "The Organizational Saga in Higher Education" *Administrative Science Quarterly* 17 (1972): 178.

11. Cheryl T. Desmond, "Comparing the Assessment of Mastery in an Outcome-based School and a Coalition of Essential Skills School" *Quality Outcomes-Driven Education* 1, no. 6 (Fall 1992): 31–38.

12. Robert C. Bogdan and Sari K. Biklen, *Qualitative Research for Education: An Introduction to Theory and Methods* (Boston: Allyn & Bacon, 1982).

13. David W. Minar, "The Community Basis of Conflict in School System

Politics," *American Sociological Review* 31 (December 1966): 822–34. Frank Lutz
and Lawrence Iannacone, *Public Participation in Local Schools* (Lexington, Mass.:
Heath, 1978). Joseph McGivney and William Moynihan, "School and Community," *Teachers College Record* 74 (December 1972): 209–24.

INTRODUCTION

1. George Korutz, interview with author, Johnson City, N.Y., 21 July 1987.
2. Seymour Sarason, *The Predictable Failure of Educational Reform* (San Francisco: Jossey-Bass, 1991).
3. Lawrence Rowe and Frank Alessi, "The Outcomes-Driven Developmental Model" (Johnson City, N.Y.: Johnson City Central School District, n.d.).
4. Ibid., 5.
5. Tom Rusk Vickery, "Excellence in an Outcome-Driven School District,"
Effective Schools Program Validation, Grant 407–84–025–038, 1985.
6. Arthur Blumberg and Phyllis Blumberg, *The School Superintendent: Living with Conflict* (New York: Teachers College Press, 1985).
7. National Commission on Excellence in Education, *A Nation at Risk*
(Washington, D.C.: U.S. Government Printing Office), 1983.
8. James Coleman, *Equality of Educational Opportunity* (Washington, D.C.:
U.S. Government Printing Office, 1966).
9. Benjamin S. Bloom, "Learning for Mastery," *Evaluation Comment*
(UCLA-CSEIP) 1, no. 2 (1968): 1–12.
10. John B. Carroll, "A Model for School Learning," *Teachers College Record*
64 (1964): 723–33.
11. For a history of mastery learning, see Thomas R. Guskey, *Implementing Mastery Learning* (Belmont, Calif.: Wadsworth, 1985).
12. Carroll developed a formula that stated that the degree of learning
was a function of perservance and the opportunity to learn divided by learning rate, quality of instruction, and ability to understand the instruction.
13. James H. Block et al., *Building Effective Mastery Learning Schools* (New
York: Longman, 1989), 6–8.
14. Ibid., 7
15. Ibid., 21–49.
16. Lynn Olson, "Chicago Scuttles Mastery-Reading Plan After $7.5 Mil-
lion, 5-Year Commitment," *Education Week*, 21 August 1985, 1, 17.
17. Block, *Building Effective Mastery Learning Schools*, 10.
18. Ibid., 11.
19. James H. Block, "On Partnerships & Great Expectations," *Outcomes* 12,
no. 4 (Winter 1993): 3.
20. "The OBE Movement Is Growing Rapidly: February Conferences
Draw Large Audiences," *Outcomes* 8, no. 1 (Winter 1989): 1.
21. Frank V. Alessi, "ODDM: The Gentle Bulldozer," *Quality Outcomes-
Driven Education* 1, no. 1 (April 1991): 11.

22. *Quality Outcomes-Driven Education* 1, no. 5 (April 1992): 64–70.

23. Ibid., 50.

24. Judith McQuaide and Ann-Maureen Pliska, "The Challenge to Pennsylvania's Education Reform," *Educational Leadership* 51, no. 4 (December 1993/January 1994): 16–21.

25. Seymour B. Sarason, *Schooling in America: Scapegoat and Salvation* (New York: The Free Press, 1983).

26. Larry Cuban, *How Teachers Taught: Constancy and Change in American Classrooms, 1890–1980* (New York: Longman, 1984), 1.

27. Ibid., 3–7.

28. Sarason, *Predictable Failure,* 123.

CHAPTER ONE

1. William Spady in James H. Block, Helen E. Efthim, and Robert B. Burns, *Building Effective Mastery Learning Schools* (New York: Longman, 1989), 12.

2. Ibid., 73.

3. William Glasser, *Control Theory in the Classroom* (New York: Harper & Row, 1986), 1–17.

4. M. Sandra Reeves, *Education Week,* 27 April 1988.

5. Larry Cuban, *How Teachers Taught: Constancy and Change in American Classrooms, 1890–1980* , 2d ed. (New York: Teachers College Press, 1993), 3.

6. See Robert F. Biehler and Jack Snowman, *Psychology Applied to Teaching* (Boston: Houghton Mifflin, 1986), 166–71, for an explanation of the measurement of intelligence in an educational psychology textbook.

7. Seymour Sarason, *The Predictable Failure of Educational Reform* (San Francisco: Jossey-Bass, 1991), 122.

8. Ibid.

9. Benjamin S. Bloom, "Learning for Mastery," *Evaluation Comment* 1, no. 2 (1968).

10. Sarason, *Predictable Failure,* 122.

11. Ibid., 124.

12. Cuban, *How Teachers Taught,* 260.

13. Gerald Grant, *The World We Created at Hamilton High* (Cambridge: Harvard University Press, 1988), 133.

CHAPTER TWO

1. Gerald Grant, *The World We Created at Hamilton High* (Cambridge: Harvard University Press, 1988), 117.

2. Ida M. Tarbell, "`Humans 90% Good' Says George F.," *Red Cross Magazine,* January 1920, 15.

3. Ibid., 17.

4. Gerald Zahavi, "Workers, Managers, and Welfare Capitalism: The Shoe-

workers and Tanners of Endicott Johnson, 1880–1950" (Ph.D. diss., Syracuse University, 1983), 63.

5. *E.J.Worker's Review*, 1 September 1919, 32-A.

6. Tarbell, "Humans," 18.

7. Richard S. Saul, "An American Entrepreneur," *Sun-Bulletin*, 5 December–23 December 1966, 4. See also Richard S. Saul, "An American Entrepreneur" (Ph.D. diss., Syracuse University, 1967).

8. *An E-J Worker's First Lesson in the Square Deal* (1922), Box 19, George F. Johnson Papers, Bird Library, Syracuse University, not paginated.

9. Tarbell, "Humans," 17.

10. Zahavi, "Workers," 129.

11. George F. Johnson, in *E.J. Workers' Review*, 20 March 1919, 1.

12, Saul, "American Entrepreneur," 13.

13. Zahavi, "Workers," 195–209.

14. Ibid., 209.

15. Saul, "American Entrepreneur," 14.

16. George F. Johnson, quoted by Tom Cawley, *Evening Press*, 5 July 1967. Neither Johnson's son George W. nor his nephew Charles F. attended college.

17. Zahavi, "Workers," 346.

18. Tarbell, "Humans," 24.

19. Robert N. Bellah et al., *Habits of the Heart: Individualism and Commitment in American Life* (New York: Harper & Row, 1985), 256.

20. Ibid.

21. Robert Owen, *The Life of Robert Owen Written by Himself, with Selections from his Writings and Correspondence*, vol. 1 (1857; New York: A. M. Kelley, 1967). Alan J. DeYoung, *Economics and American Education* (New York: Longman, 1989), 16.

22. Owen, *Life of Robert Owen*, 302.

23. Tarbell, "Humans," 15.

24. Bellah et al., *Habits of the Heart*, 256.

25. Ibid., 254.

26. Ibid., 260.

27. Ibid.

28. Harold W. Stevenson and James W. Stigler, *The Learning Gap: Why Our Schools Are Failing and What We Can Learn from Japanese and Chinese Education* (New York: Summit Books, 1992).

CHAPTER THREE

1. George Korutz, interview with author, Johnson City, New York, 22 July 1987.

2. William Rodgers, *Think: A Biography of the Watsons and IBM* (New York: Stein and Day, 1969), 217. The Rodgers biography is considered an unofficial biography of Watson. Thomas J. Watson Sr. and his family cooperated with

Thomas G. Belden and Marva R. Belden for *The Lengthening Shadow: The Life of Thomas J. Watson* (Boston: Little, Brown, 1962).

3. Belden and Belden, *Lengthening Shadow,* 89–93.

4. Rodgers, *Think,* 55.

5. Belden and Belden, *Lengthening Shadow,* 127.

6. Ibid.

7. Richard S. Saul, "An American Entrepreneur," *Sun-Bulletin,* 5–23 December 1966, 23.

8. Belden and Belden, *Lengthening Shadow,* 141.

9. Rodgers, *Think.*

10. Saul, "American Entrepreneur," 22.

11. Belden and Belden, *Lengthening Shadow,* 152.

12. Rodgers, *Think,* 93.

13. Saul, "American Entrepreneur," 21.

14. James S. Coleman and Thomas Hoffer, *Public and Private High Schools: The Impact of Communities* (New York: Basic Books, 1987), 5–6.

15. U.S. Bureau of the Census, *U.S. Census of Population and Housing, 1960* (Washington, D.C.: U.S. Government Printing Office).

16. Michael G. Fullan, *The New Meaning of Educational Change,* 2d ed. (New York: Teachers College Press, 1991), 58.

17. *Sun-Bulletin,* 23 March 1986.

18. "Village of Johnson City Comprehensive Development Plan, 1967" (Binghamton, N.Y.: Broome County Planning Office), EB6.

19. Ibid., P-3.

20. David B. Tyack, *The One Best System: A History of American Urban Education* (Cambridge: Harvard University Press, 1974). David B. Tyack and Elisabeth Hansot, *Managers of Virtue: Public School Leadership in America, 1820–1980* (New York: Basic Books, 1982), 253.

21. James Bryant Conant, *The American High School Today* (New York: McGraw-Hill, 1959). In this book, Conant recommends a drastic reduction in the number of small high schools through district reorganization and the construction of comprehensive high schools.

22. *Sun-Bulletin,* 12 October 1961.

23. *Sun-Bulletin,* 21 May 1964.

24. Ibid.

25. Alan Peshkin, *Growing Up American: Schooling and the Survival of Community* (Chicago: University of Chicago Press, 1978), 200.

26. Coleman and Hoffer, *Public and Private High Schools,* 7.

27. Joseph H. McGivney and William Moynihan, "School and Community," *Teachers College Record* 74, no. 2 (December 1972). Their typology of school-community relationships predicts that rapidly changing socioeconomic conditions such as the rise or fall of overall community income or educational attainment, increased or decreased property valuation, rapid development of real estate, or significant population migrations will cause sufficient social dis-

sonance in the community to create conflict within the community-school relationship and lead to a demand for educational change from residents. Community-school conflict will also occur when external mandates, such as federal and state regulations and court decisions, or when the actions of professional reformers are imposed upon the community without local agreement and are incompatible with the dominant community ethos.

CHAPTER FOUR

1. *Sun-Bulletin*, 21 May 1964.
2. Robert N. Bellah et al., *Habits of the Heart: Individualism and Commitment in American Life* (New York: Harper & Row, 195), 170–171.
3. Alexis de Tocqueville, *Democracy in America*, trans. George Lawrence, ed. J. P. Mayer and Max Lerner (New York: Harper & Row, 1966), 497.
4. Ibid., 499.
5. Bellah et al., *Habits of the Heart*, 175.
6. John Dewey, *The Public and Its Problems* (Denver, Colo.: Alan Swallow, 1937), 38–39.
7. Ibid., 147.
8. Ibid., 76.
9. Bellah et al., *Habits of the Heart*, 188.
10. David Luzadis, interview with author, Greene, N.Y., 2 December 1988.
11. Ibid.
12. James Ballus, interview with author, Johnson City, N.Y., 7 November 1988.
13. Luzadis interview.
14. Ibid.
15. *Sun-Bulletin*, 17 June 1964.
16. David Tyack and Elisabeth Hansot, *Managers of Virtue: Public School Leadership in America, 1820–1980* (New York: Basic Books, 1982), 160–66.
17. Ibid., 163.
18. Samuel Goldman, *The Report of a Survey of the Johnson City Central School District* (Syracuse, N.Y.: Bureau of School Service, School of Education, Syracuse University, July 1966), 38.
19. Ibid., 189.
20. Ibid., 190.
21. Ibid., 188.
22. Ibid., 13.
23. "The Basic Curriculum, Grades 7–12, Johnson City Central School District," Minutes, 26 September 1966, 21.
24. Johnson City Central School District Minutes, 13 March 1968.
25. Arthur J. Vidich and Joseph Bensman, *Small Town in Mass Society*, 2d ed. (1958; Princeton: Princeton University Press, 1968), 332.
26. Bellah et al., *Habits of the Heart*, 188–190, 208–11.

27. Ibid., 188.
28. Ibid., 189.
29. de Tocqueville, *Democracy in America,* 668.

CHAPTER FIVE

1. *The American Heritage Dictionary of the English Language*e, 3d ed. (Boston: Houghton Mifflin, 1992), 979.
2. Christopher Hodgkinson, *Educational Leadership: The Moral Art* (Albany, N.Y.: State University of New York Press, 1991), 36.
3. Ibid., 81.
4. Lawrence A. Cremin, *The Transformation of the School: Progressivism in American Education, 1876–1957* (New York: Vintage Books, 1964), 302.
5. Johnson City Central School District Minutes, 25 May 1971.
6. John R. Champlin, interview with author, Syracuse, New York, 6 May 1988.
7. Minutes, September 1971.
8. Minutes, 14 December 1971.
9. Minutes, 23 November 1971.
10. Champlin interview.
11. Ibid.
12. Hodgkinson, *Educational Leadership,* 44.
13. *Sun-Bulletin,* 10 May 1972.
14. Minutes, 23 May 1972.
15. John Bell, interview with author, Johnson City, N.Y., 19 April 1989. A similar statement was also made by John Shelton, interview with author, Johnson City, N.Y., 21 July 1987.
16. Minutes, 13 June 1973.
17. *Evening Press,* 16 July 1973.
18. Edward Radin, interview with author, Johnson City, N.Y., 20 July 1987.
19. Laurence Iannacone and Frank Lutz, *Politics, Power, and Policy* (Columbus, Ohio: Charles E. Merrill Pub. Co., 1970), ix.
20. Superintendent Champlin's support folder prepared for the school board, 5 March 1976.
21. John R. Champlin, interview with author, Syracuse, N.Y., 6 May 1988.
22. Thomas Jablonowski, interview with author, Binghamton, N.Y., 3 August 1989.
23. Minutes, 8 January 1980.
24. The district was featured in articles by the *New York Times* on 16 October 1980, by *Family Circle* on 17 March 1981, and by several state and national educational publications.
25. Champlin was the 1982 recipient of the American Association of School Administrators "Leadership for Learning" Award and recognized at several conferences that year.

26. Hodgkinson, *Educational Leadership*, 113.
27. Ibid.
28. Ibid.
29. Ibid.
30. Ibid., 43.
31. See chapter 10 for a detailed exploration of this conflict.

CHAPTER SIX

1. Ron Brandt, "Is Outcome-Based Education Dead?" *Educational Leadership*, March 1994, 5.
2. Barnett Berry and Rick Ginsberg, "Effective Schools, Teachers, and Principals: Today's Evidence, Tomorrow's Prospects," in *Educational Leadership and Changing Contexts of Families, Communities, and Schools,* eds. Brad Mitchell and Luvern L. Cunningham. Eighty-ninth Yearbook of the National Society for the Study of Education, (Chicago: University of Chicago, 1990), 2: 155.
3. See W. Edwards Deming, *Out of the Crisis* (Cambridge: MIT Press, 1986) for an extensive explanation of his fourteen principles.
4. Brad Mitchell, "Children, Youth, and Restructured Schools: Views from the Field," in *Educational Leadership and Changing Contexts* , 2:54.
5. John Dewey, *Education Today* (New York: G. P. Putnam's Sons, 19840), 67.
6. Theodore R. Sizer, *Horace's Compromise: The Dilemma of the American High School* (Boston: Houghton Mifflin, 1984), 184.
7. Mitchell, "Children, Youth," 56.
8. Seth Kreisberg, *Transforming Power: Domination, Empowerment, and Education* (Albany: State University of New York Press, 1992), 21.
9. Ibid., 20.
10. Ibid., 6.
11. See Thomas J. Sergiovanni, "Adding Value to Leadership Gets Extraordinary Results," *Educational Leadership* 97, no. 8 (May 1990): 23–27.
12. *Educational Leadership and Changing Contexts..*
13. Sharon Rallis, "Professional Teachers and Restructured Schools: Leadership Challenges" in ibid., 2:201.
14. John Champlin, "Johnson City: One Retrospective," *Outcomes* 12, no. 4, (Winter 1993): 30–34.
15. Michael J. Schmoker and Richard B. Wilson, *Total Quality Education* (Bloomington, Ind.: Phi Delta Kappa Educational Foundation, 1993), 11, 37–66.
16. William Glasser, *The Quality School: Managing Students Without Coercion* (New York: Harper & Row, 1990), 92, 154.
17. Ibid., 11.
18. Ibid., 32.
19. Albert Mamary, "The Outcomes-Driven Developmental Model," document distributed at ODDM conference, Binghamton, N.Y., 1987.

20. Ibid., 3.

21. Christopher Hodgkinson, *Educational Leadership: The Moral Art* (Albany: State University of New York Press, 1991), 50. Donald A. Schon, *The Reflective Turn: Case Studies In and On Educational Practice* (New York: Teachers College Press, 1991).

22. Seymour B. Sarason, *The Predictable Failure of Educational Reform* (San Francisco: Jossey-Bass, 1991), 26.

23. Paulo Freire, *Pedagogy of the Oppressed* (New York: Continuum, 1970), 57–65.

24. Ibid., 65.

25. Kreisberg, *Transforming Power*, 35.

26. Ibid., 37

27. Ibid., 45.

28. Ibid., 51.

29. Richard Katz, cited in ibid.

30. John R. Champlin, "Leadership: A Change Agent's View," *Quality Outcomes-Driven Education* 3, no. 3 (February 1994): 9–10.

31. Freire, *Pedagogy*, 67

32. Ibid., 71.

33. Kreisberg, *Transforming Power*, 85–86.

34. Richard Katz cited in ibid., 80–81.

35. Ibid., 81.

36. Champlin, *Leadership*, 11.

37. Ibid., 12.

38. James D. Marshall, "Foucault and Education," *Australian Journal of Education* 33, no. 2 (1989): 99–113.

39. Michel Foucault, "The Subject and Power," in Hubert L. Dreyfus and Paul Rabinow, *Michel Foucault: Beyond Structuralism and Hermeneutics*, 2d ed. (Chicago: University of Chicago Press, 1983), 220.

40. Michel Foucault, *Power/Knowledge: Selected Interviews and Other Writings, 1972–1977* (New York: Pantheon, 1980), 52.

41. Michel Foucault, *The Archaeology of Knowledge and the Discourse on Language* (New York: Pantheon, 1972), 107–8.

42. Ibid., 38.

43. Johnson City Central School District Minutes, 13 June 1973.

44. Ibid.

45. Champlin, "Leadership," 10.

46. Ibid., 220.

47. Michel Foucault, *The History of Sexuality* (New York; Pantheon, 1978), 1:101.

48. Wilfrid Carr and Stephen Kemmis, *Becoming Critical: Knowing Through Action Research* (Victoria: Deakin University, 1983), cited in Peter McLaren, *Life in Schools* (New York: Longman, 1989), 167.

CHAPTER SEVEN

1. John R. Champlin, "Leadership: A Change Agent's View," *Quality Outcomes-Driven Education* 3, no. 3 (February 1994): 10.
2. Ibid.
3. John R. Champlin, *Outcomes Drive the System: An ODDM Primer* (Fountain Hills, Ariz.: National Center for Outcome-Based Education), 8.
4. Ibid., 10.
5. Richard Katz, 1982, cited in Seth Kreisberg, *Transforming Power: Domination, Empowerment, and Education* (Albany: State University of New York Press, 1992), 78.
6. Johnson City Central School District Minutes, 16 November 1976.
7. Minutes, 22 January 1974.
8. Ibid.
9. Ibid.
10. Minutes with attached curriculum report, "Project Redesign," 8 March 1977.
11. *New York Times*, 16 November 1980l. Reprinted by permission.
12. Tom Rusk Vickery, keynote address, Outcomes Driven Developmental Model Conference, Binghamton, N.Y., 1987.
13. *Sun-Bulletin*, 10 May 1972.
14. Minutes, 23 May 1972.
15. Minutes, 23 October 1973.
16. Johnson City Central School District School Board Support Folder, prepared by superintendent John R. Champlin, 11 April 1978.
17. John R. Champlin, "A Study and Analysis of Factors Influencing Testing and Learning in the Johnson City Central School District," Minutes, 11 April 1978.
18. School Board Support Folder, prepared by Superintendent John R. Champlin, 22 August 1978.
19. *New York Times*, 16 November 1980.
20. Ibid.
21. Anthony Brandt, "The School Where Everyone Gets A's," *Family Circle*, 17 March 1981, reprint, 1–3.
22. Ibid., 1–2.
23. Ibid., 3.

CHAPTER EIGHT

1. Michel Foucault, *Power/knowledge: Selected Interviews and Other Writings, 1972–1977* (New York: Pantheon, 1980), 93.
2. Champlin, "Leadership, A Change Agent's View," *Quality Outcomes-Driven Education* 3, no. 3 (February 1994): 10.
3. John R. Champlin, interview with author, Syracuse, N.Y., 6 May 1988.

4. Sara Lawrence Lightfoot, *The Good High School* (New York: Basic Books, 1983), 329.

5. Edward Radin, interview with author, Johnson City, N.Y., 20 July 1987; William Kingsley, interview with author, Johnson City, N.Y., 22 July 1987; David Luzadis, interview with author, Greene, N.Y., 2 December 1988.

6. Mary Parker Follett, *Creative Experience* (New York: Longman, 1924), xii.

7. Nancy J. Smith, "Reconsiderations of Dynamic Administration: The Collected Papers of Mary Parker Follett," *Educational Studies* 25, no. 3 (Fall 1994): 201

8. Ibid., 202.

9. Ibid.

10. Seth Kreisberg, *Transforming Power: Domination, Empowerment, and Education* (Albany: State University of New York Press, 1992), 73.

11. Follett, *Creative Experience*, 196.

12. Smith, "Reconsiderations," 9.

13. Ibid., 3.

14. Ibid., 12.

15. Mary Parker Follett, cited in Smith, "Reconsiderations," 12.

16. Mary Parker Follett, *Dynamic Administration: The Collected Papers of Mary Parker Follett*, ed. Henry C. Metcalf and Lyndall Urwick (New York: Harper & Brothers, 1944), 297.

17. Johnson City Central School District Minutes, 14 December 1982.

18. Ron Brandt, "On Creating an Environment Where All Students Learn: A Conversation with Al Mamary," *Educational Leadership* 51, no. 6 (March 1994): 24–25.

19. John R. Champlin and Albert Mamary, "Johnson City's Philosophical Principles and Practices," *Outcomes* 2, no. 1 (1982): 22–23.

20. Tom Rusk Vickery, "Excellence in an Outcomes-Driven School District," Effective Schools Program Validation, Grant 407–84–02–025–038, September 1985.

21. Lawrence Rowe and Frank V. Alessi, "The Outcomes-Driven Developmental Model" (Johnson City: Johnson City Central School District, 1993), 3.

22. Tom Rusk Vickery, keynote address, Outcomes Driven Developmental Conference, Binghamton, N.Y., 1987.

23. Ibid.

24. Minutes, 14 November 1978.

25. William Glasser, *Control Theory in the Classroom* (New York: Harper & Row, 1986).

26. Rowe and Alessi, "Outcomes-Driven Developmental Model," 22–26.

27. Glasser, *Control Theory*, 17.

28. Ibid.

29. Ibid., 19.

30. Ibid., 20.

31. Ibid., 23.

32. Ibid., 24.

33. Ibid., 63.

34. These passages are excerpts of Glasser's full explanations of these principles contained in his article "The Quality School" *Quality Outcomes-Driven Education* 1, no. 2 (October 1991): 57–66. See William Glasser, *The Quality School: Managing Students Without Coercion* (New York: Harper & Row, 1990).

CHAPTER NINE

1. Starhawk, *Dreaming the Dark: Magic, Sex, and Politics* (Boston: Beacon Press, 1988), 3.

2. Johnson City Central School District School Board Minutes, 10 March 1970. Program for team teaching at the high school. Minutes also report that one-third of the district's eleventh-grade students fell below the state's average percentile in reading. District efforts to improve schools at the elementary level are reported in the 20 December 1970, 26 January 1971, and 23 February 1971 Minutes. One of these programs was titled "Impacts: Individualizing Materials Permitting All Children to Succeed."

3. Tom Rusk Vickery, "Learning From an Outcomes-Driven School District," *Educational Leadership* 45 (Spring 88): 52–56.

4. Albert Mamary, interview with author, Johnson City, N.Y., 17 March 1986.

5. Vickery, "Learning," 56.

6. Ibid., 55.

7. Alexandre Kojève, *Introduction to the Reading of Hegel* (New York: Basic Books, 1969), 42.

8. Ibid., 16–17, 25.

9. Fred Newman and Lois Holzman, *Lev Vygotsky: Revolutionary Scientist* (New York: Routledge, 1993). Vygotsky was and is best known as a psychologist, scientist, theoretician, but he was also a teacher and an artist during his short thirty-seven years. See L. S. Vygotsky, *Mind in Society: The Development of Higher Psychological Processes*, ed. Michael Cole et al. (Cambridge: Harvard University Press, 1978).

10. Vygotsky, *Mind in Society*, 7.

11. Starhawk, *Dreaming the Dark*, 24.

12, Ibid.

13. Barbara Z. Presseisen and Alex Kozulin, "Mediated Learning—The Contributions of Vygotsky and Feuerstein in Theory and Practice." Paper presented at the annual meeting of the American Educational Research Association, San Francisco, April 1992, 1.

14. Reuven Feuerstein and S. Feuerstein, "Mediated Learning Experience: A Theoretical Review," in Reuven Feuerstein et al., *Mediated Learning Experience (MLE): Theoretical, Psychological, and Learning Implications* (London: Freund, 1991), 5.

15. Cited in Presseisen and Kozulin, "Mediated Learning," 7.

16. Ibid., 15.

17. Kozulin, cited in Presseisen and Kozulin, "Mediated Learning, 13.

18. Ibid.

19. Ibid., 14.

20. Ibid., 6–7.

21. J. A. Kulik, C. C. Kulik, and P. A. Cohen, "A Meta-Analysis of Outcome Studies of Keller's Personalized System of Instruction," *American Psychologist* 34 (1979): 307–18

22. Daniel Levine and Robert Havighurst, *Society and Education*, 6th ed. (Boston: Allyn and Bacon, 1980).

23. David C. McClelland, *Power: The Inner Experience* (New York: Irvington, 1975), 85–86.

24. Jean Baker Miller, *Toward a New Psychology of Women* (Boston: Beacon Press, 1976), 83.

25. Ibid., 171.

26. Nel Noddings, "An Ethic of Caring and Its Implications for Instructional Arrangements," in *The Education Feminism Reader*, edited by Lynda Stone. (New York: Routledge, 1994), 174. See also Nel Noddings, *Caring: A Feminine Approach to Ethics & Moral Education* (Berkeley: University of California Press, 1984).

28. Noddings, "An Ethic," 174.

29. Tom Rusk Vickery, "Evaluating a Mastery Learning High School," *Persoon En Gemeenschap* 40, no. 10 (1987/88): 803.

CHAPTER TEN

1. Lawrence Rowe and Frank V. Alessi, "The Outcomes-Driven Developmental Model" (Johnson City, N.Y.: Johnson City Central School District, n.d.).

2. Karen M. Evans and Jean A. King, "Research on OBE: What We Know and Don't Know," *Educational Leadership* 51, no. 6 (March 1994): 13–14.

3. Tom Rusk Vickery, "Evaluating a Mastery Learning High School," *Person en Gemeeschap* 40, no. 10 (1987/88): 801.

4. Ibid., 802.

5. U.S. Department of Commerce, *Statistical Abstract of the United States* (Washington: U.S. Government Printing Office, 1993).

6. Rowe and Alessi, "Outcomes-Driven Developmental Model," 7.

7. The procedures and components are extensively outlined in ibid, 13.

8. Ibid., 16.

9. William G. Spady, "Choosing Outcomes of Significance," *Educational Leadership* 51, no. 6 (March 1994): 18–22.

10. Partners for Quality Learning, National Center for Outcome-Based Education Division, Syracuse, N.Y.

11. Evans and King, "Research on OBE," 12–17.

12. Terry P. Applegate and W. Keith Evans, "ODDM in Utah" (Salt Lake City: Utah State Office of Education, 1994), 10–11.

13. Evans and King, "Research on OBE," 16.

14. *Education Week*, 13 October 1993.

15. *New York Times*, 9 January 1994.

16. David Hill, "Christian Soldier," *Teacher Magazine*, November/December 1992, 18–21.

17. Ibid, 18. Also see Robert L. Simonds, "A Plea for the Children," *Educational Leadership* 51, no. 4 (December 1993/January 1994): 12–15.

18. Nancy Staible, Citizens for Excellence in Education, directive to CEE Members Nationwide, 1992.

19. Judith McQuaide and Ann-Maureen Pliska, "The Challenge to Pennsylvania's Education Reform," *Educational Leadership* 51, no. 4 (December 1993/January 1994): 16–21. Also see Ann-Maureen Pliska and Judith McQuaide, "Pennsylvania's Battle for Student Learning Outcomes," *Educational Leadership* 51, no. 6 (March 1994): 66–69, and Arnold Burron, "Traditionalist Christians and OBE: What's the Problem?" *Educational Leadership* 51, no. 6 (March 1994): 73–75.

20. Joel Spring, *American Education* (New York: McGraw-Hill, 1994), 268.

21. See the Alpha-Omega Curriculum, Christian Educational Supplies, P.O. Box 3153, Tempe, Ariz. 85280.

22. Rich Kirkpatrick, "State grants final approval to OBE; challenge likely," *Intelligencer Journal*, 6 May 1993.

23. *New York Times*, 9 January 1994.

24. Robert A. Frahm, "The Failure of Connecticut's Reform Plan," *Phi Delta Kappan* 71, no. 2 (October 1994): 156–59.

25. Ibid., 157.

26. Ibid., 158.

27. Simone Weil, *The Need for Roots* (Boston: Beacon Press, 1952), 300.

Bibliography

Alessi, Frank V. "ODDM: The Gentle Bulldozer." *Quality Outcomes-Driven Education* 1, no. 1 (April 1991): 11.

Allison, Derek J. "Toward an Improved Understanding of the Organizational Nature of Schools." *Educational Administration Quarterly* 19 (Fall 1983): 7–34.

Alvey, Donald T., and Kenneth E. Underwood. "When Boards and Superintendents Clash, It's Over the Balance of School Power." *The American School Board Journal* 172 (1985): 21–25.

Apple, Michael. *Education and Power*. Boston: Routledge & Kegan Paul, 1982.

Applegate, Terry P., and W. Keith Evans. "ODDM in Utah." Salt Lake City: Utah State Office of Education, 1994.

Avender, Michael. "The Superintendent–School Board Relationship." *Canadian Journal of Education* 10 (Spring 1985): 176–98.

Bacharach, Samuel B. *Consensus and Power in School Organizations*. Ithaca, N.Y.: Cornell University (ERIC Document Reproduction Service No. ED 243 174), 1983.

Baldridge, J. Victor, and Terrence E. Deal, eds. *Managing Changes in Educational Organizations: Sociological Perspectives, Strategies, and Case Studies*. Berkeley, Calif.: McCutchan Publishing Co., 1975.

"The Basic Curriculum, Grades 7–12, Johnson City Central School District." Johnson City Central School District Board Minutes, 26 September, 1966.

Belden, Thomas G., and Marva R. Belden. *The Lengthening Shadow: The Life of Thomas J. Watson*. Boston: Little, Brown, 1962.

Bellah, Robert N., Richard Madsen, William M Sullivan, Ann Swidler, and Steven M. Tipton. *Habits of the Heart: Individualism and Commitment in American Life*. New York: Harper and Row, 1985.

Bennis, Warren. *Changing Organizations*. New York: McGraw-Hill, 1966.

Berman, Paul, and Milbrey W. McLaughlin. "Implementation of Educational

Innovation." *The Educational Forum* 40 (March 1976): 345–70.

Berry, Barnett, and Rick Ginsberg. "Effective Schools, Teachers, and Principals: Today's Evidence, Tomorrow's Prospects." In pt. 2 of *Educational
Leadership and Changing Contexts of Families, Communities, and Schools,*
edited by Brad Mitchell and Luvern L. Cunningham. Eighty-ninth Yearbook of the National Society for the Study of Education. Chicago: University of Chicago, 1990.

Binghamton-Johnson City Directory. Bellows Falls, Vt.: H. A. Manning Co., 1982.

Block, James H., ed. *Schools, Society, and Mastery Learning.* New York: Holt,
Reinhart and Winston, 1974.

Block, James H. "On Partnerships and Great Expectations." *Outcomes* 12, no. 4
(Winter 1993): 3.

Bloom, Benjamin S. *All Our Children Learning: A Primer for Parents, Teachers,
and Other Educators.* New York: McGraw-Hill, 1981.

———. *Human Characteristics and School Learning.* New York: McGraw-Hill,
1976.

———. "Learning for Mastery." *UCLA Evaluation Comment* 1, no. 2 (May
1968).

Blumberg, Arthur, and Phyllis Blumberg. *The School Superintendent.* New York:
Teachers College Press, 1985.

Bogdan, Robert C., and Sari K. Biklen. *Qualitative Research for Education: An
Introduction to Theory and Methods.* Boston: Allyn & Bacon, 1982.

Boyd, William L. "The Changing Politics of Curriculum Policy Making for
American Schools." *Review of Educational Research* 48 (1978): 577–628.

———. "Community Status, Citizen Participation and Conflict in Suburban
School Politics." Ph.D. diss., University of Chicago, 1973.

———. "The Public, the Professionals, and Educational Policy Making: Who
Governs?" *Teachers College Record* 77 (May 1976): 539–77.

———. "Rethinking Educational Policy and Management: Political Science
and Educational Administration in the 1980s." *American Journal of Education* 92 (November 1983): 20–29.

———. "The Study of Educational Policy and Politics: Much Ado About Noth-
ing." *Teachers College Record* 80(December 1978): 80.

Brandt, Anthony. "The School Where Everyone Gets A's." *Family Circle,* 17
March 1981, reprint, 1–3.

Brandt, Ron. "Is Outcome-Based Education Dead?" *Educational Leadership* 51,
no. 6 (March 1994): 5.

———. "On Creating an Environment Where All Students Learn: A Conversation with Al Mamary." *Educational Leadership* 51, no. 6 (March 1994):
24–25.

Broome County Chamber of Commerce. "Some Significant Dates in the History of Broome County New York." Binghamton, N.Y.: The Chamber, n.d.

Budin, Morris, John W. Frazier, and Lucius S. Willis. *Population Analysis of
Johnson City, New York.* Binghamton, N.Y.: Department of Geography,

SUNY-Binghamton, June 1986.

Burbules, Nicholas C. "A Theory of Power in Education." *Educational Theory* 36 (Spring 1986): 95–114.

Burns, Robert. *Models of Instructional Organization: A Casebook on Mastery Learning and Outcome-Based Education.* Contract number 400–86–0009. Washington, D.C.: U. S. Department of Education, April 1987.

Burron, Arnold. "Traditionalist Christians and OBE: What's the Problem?" *Educational Leadership* 51 (March 1994): 73–75.

Callahan, Raymond E. *Education and the Cult of Efficiency.* Chicago: University of Chicago Press, 1962.

Campbell, Roald, et al. *The Organization and Control of American Schools.* Columbus, Ohio: Charles Merrill, 1980.

Canizares, Anita M., and Tom Rusk Vickery. "Principals' Perceptions of Teachers' Instructional Practices: A Case Study." Paper presented at the annual meeting of the American Educational Research Association, New Orleans, La., April 1988.

Carnoy, Martin, and Levin, Henry M. *The Limits of Educational Reform.* New York: David McKay, 1976.

————. *School and Work in the Democratic State.* Stanford, Calif.: Stanford University Press, 1985.

Carr, Wilfrid, and Stephen Kemmis. *Becoming Critical: Knowing Through Action Research.* Victoria, B.C.: Deakin University, 1983.

Carroll, John B. "A Model for School Learning." *Teachers College Record* 64 (1963): 723–33.

Champlin, John R. "Johnson City: One Retrospective." *Outcomes* 12, no. 4 (Winter 1993): 30–34.

————. "Johnson City Central School District School Board Support Folder." 11 April 1978.

————. "Johnson City Central School District School Board Support Folder." 22 August 1978.

————. "Leadership: A Change Agent's View." *Quality Outcomes-Driven Education* 3, no. 3 (February 1994): 9–10.

————. *Outcomes Drive the System: An ODDM Primer.* Fountain Hills, Ariz.: National Center for Outcome Based Education, n.d.

————. "A Study and Analysis of Factors Influencing Testing and Learning in the Johnson City Central School District." Johnson City Central School District Board Minutes. 11 April 1978.

Champlin, John R., and Albert Mamary. "Johnson City's Philosophical Principles and Practices." *Outcomes* 2, no. 1 (1982): 22–23

Charters, W. W., Jr., "Social Class Analysis and the Control of Public Education." *Harvard Educational Review* 24 (Autumn 1953): 268.

Cistone, Peter J. "The Socialization of Board Members." *Educational Administration Quarterly* 13:2 (1977): 19–23.

————, ed. *Understanding School Boards.* Lexington, Mass: Heath & Co., 1975.

Clark, Burton R. "The Organizational Saga in Higher Education." *Administrative Science Quarterly* 17, no. 2 (1972): 178–84.

Clark, David L., Linda S. Lotto, and Terry A. Astuto. "Effective Schools and School Improvement: A Comparative Analysis of Two Lines of Inquiry." *Educational Administrative Quarterly* 20 (Summer 1984): 41–68.

Cohen, David K. "Reforming School Politics." *Harvard Educational Review* 48 (November 1978): 429–47.

Coleman, James. *Equality of Educational Opportunity.* Washington, D.C.: U.S. Government Printing Office, 1966.

Coleman, James and Thomas Hoffer. *Public and Private High Schools: The Impact of Communities.* New York: Basic Books, 1987.

Conant, James Bryant. *The American High School Today.* New York: McGraw-Hill, 1959.

Corbett, H. Dickson, et al. *School Context and School Change: Implications for Effective Planning.* New York: Teachers College Press, 1984.

Corwin, Ronald G. *A Sociology of Education: Emerging Class, Status, and Power in the Public Schools.* New York: Appleton-Century-Crofts, 1965.

Counts, George S. *The Social Composition of Boards of Education.* 1927. Reprint, New York: Arno Press, 1969.

Cremin, Lawrence A. *The Transformation of the School: Progressivism in American Education, 1876–1957.* New York: Vintage Books, 1964.

Cuban, Larry. *How Teachers Taught: Constancy and Change in American Classrooms, 1890–1980.* 2d ed. New York: Teachers College Press, 1993.

———. *Urban School Chiefs Under Fire.* Chicago: University of Chicago Press, 1976.

Cubberly, Ellwood. *Public Education in the United States.* Boston: Houghton Mifflin, 1919.

Daft, Richard, and Selwyn W. Becker. *The Innovative Organization: Innovation Adoption in School Organizations.* New York: Elsevier, 1978.

Dahl, Robert A. *Modern Political Analysis.* Englewood Cliffs, N.J.: Prentice-Hall, 1970.

———. *Who Governs? Democracy and Power in an American City.* New Haven: Yale University Press, 1961.

Danis, Ruth. "Policy Changes in Local Schools: The Dissatisfaction Theory of Democracy." *Urban Education* 19, no. 2 (1984): 125–44.

Danzberger, J. P., et al. "The Forgotten Players on the Educational Team." *Phi Delta Kappan* 69 (September 1987): 53–59.

Desmond, Cheryl T. "Comparing the Assessment of Mastery in an Outcome-based School and a Coalition of Essential Skills School." *Quality Outcomes-Driven Education* 1, no. 6 (Fall 1992): 31–38.

———. "An Historical Analysis of the Dynamics of School and Community Reform." Ph.D. diss., Syracuse University, 1990.

Dewey, John. *Education Today.* New York: G. P. Putnam's Sons, 1984.

———. *The Public and Its Problems.* Denver, Colo.: Alan Swallow, 1937.

DeYoung, Alan J. *Economics and American Education*. New York: Longman, 1989.

Doyle, Denis P., and Chester E. Finn Jr., "American Schools and the Future of Local Control." *The Public Interest*, 1983, 77–95.

Dreyfus, Hubert L., and Paul Rabinow. *Michel Foucault: Beyond Structuralism and Hermeneutics*. 2d ed. Chicago: University of Chicago Press, 1983.

Dykes, Archie. *School Board and Superintendent: Their Effective Working Relationships*. Danville, Ill.: Interstate, 1965.

Easton, David. *A Framework for Political Analysis*. Englewood Cliffs, N.J.: Prentice-Hall, 1965.

Eblen, David R. "School District Conflict and Superintendent Turnover in Transitional Suburban Communities." Ph.D. diss., University of Chicago, 1975.

Edmonds, Ronald R., and J. R. Frederiksen. *Search for Effective Schools: The Identification and Analysis of City Schools that are Instructionally Effective for Poor Children*. Cambridge: Center for Urban Studies, Harvard University, 1979.

An E-J Worker's First Lesson in the Square Deal. Box 19, George F. Johnson Papers, Bird Library, Syracuse University, 1922.

E.J. Worker's Review. 1 September 1919.

Evans, Karen M., and Jean A. King. "Research on OBE: What We Know and Don't Know." *Educational Leadership* 51, no. 6 (March 1994): 13–14.

Feuerstein, Reuven, and S. Feuerstein, "Mediated Learning Experience: A Theoretical Review." In *Mediated Learning Experience (MLE): Theoretical, Psychological, and Learning Implications*, edited by Reuven Feuerstein and S. Feuerstein. London: Freund, 1991.

Follett, Mary Parker. *Creative Experience*. New York: Longman, 1924.

———. *Dynamic Administration: The Collected Papers of Mary Parker Follett*. Edited by Henry C. Metcalf and Lyndall Urwick. New York: Harper & Brothers, 1944.

Foucault, Michel. *The Archaeology of Knowledge and the Discourse on Language*. New York: Pantheon Books, 1972.

———. *The History of Sexuality*. Vol. 1., *An Introduction*. New York: Pantheon Books, 1978.

———. *Power/knowledge: Selected Interviews and Other Writings, 1972–1977*. New York: Pantheon Books, 1980.

———. "The Subject and Power." Afterword in *Michel Foucault: Beyond Structuralism and Hermeneutics*, by Herbert L. Dreyfus and Paul Rabinow. 2d ed. Chicago: University of Chicago Press, 1983.

Frahm, Robert A. "The Failure of Connecticut's Reform Plan." *Phi Delta Kappan* 71, no. 2 (October 1994): 156–59.

Frail, Jennie. "The Jennie Frail History." In the Your Home Library collection. Johnson City, N.Y., 1952.

Freeborn, Robert M. "School Board Changes and the Succession Patterns of Superintendents." Ph.D. diss., Claremont Graduate School, 1966.

Freire, Paulo. *Pedagogy of the Oppressed*. New York: Continuum, 1970.

Fullan, Michael G. *The Meaning of Educational Change*. New York: Teachers College Press, 1982.

———. *The New Meaning of Educational Change*. 2d ed. New York: Teachers College Press, 1991.

Fullan, Michael G., et al. "Support Systems for Implementing Curriculum in School Boards." Toronto: Ontario Institute for Studies in Education (ERIC Document Reproduction Service No. ED 276 110), 1986.

Fuller, Wayne E. *The Old Country School*. Chicago: University of Chicago Press, 1982.

Garberina, William L. "Public Demand, School Board Response and Incumbent Defeat: An Explanation of the Governance of Local School Districts in Massachusetts." Ph.D. diss., Pennsylvania State University, 1975.

Garms, Walter I., et al. *School Finance: The Economics and Politics of Public Education*. Englewood Cliffs, N.J.: Prentice-Hall, 178.

Giroux, Henry A. *Ideology, Culture, and the Process of Schooling*. Philadelphia: Temple Univrsity Press, 1981.

———. *Schooling and the Struggle for Public Life: Critical Pedagogy in the Modern Age*. Minneapolis: University of Minnesota Press, 1988.

Glasser, William. *Control Theory in the Classroom*. New York: Harper and Row, 1986.

———. "The Quality School." *Quality Outcomes-Driven Education* 1, no. 2 (October 1991): 57–66.

———. *The Quality School: Managing Students Without Coercion*. New York: Harper and Row, 1990.

———. "Reality Therapy: An Anti-Failure Approach." *Impact* 2 (1972): 6–9.

Godfrey, Margaret, and Swanchak, John. "How Compatible? Board of Education's Power and Politics of Education." Paper presented at the annual meeting of the Eastern Educational Research Association, Virginia Beach, Va., February 1985.

Gold, Barry A., and M. B. Miles. *Whose School Is It, Anyway? Parent Teacher Conflict over an Innovation School*. New York: Praeger, 1981.

Goldhammer, Keith. *The School Board*. New York: The Center for Applied Research in Education, Inc., 1964.

Goldman, Samuel. *The Report of a Survey of the Johnson City Central School District*. Syracuse, N.Y.: Bureau of School Service, School of Education, Syracuse University, July 1966.

Goodlad, John T., ed. *The Ecology of School Renewal*. Eighty-Sixth Yearbook of the National Society for the Study of Education, part 1. Chicago: University of Chicago Press, 1987.

Grant, Gerald. *The World We Created at Hamilton High*. Cambridge: Harvard University Press, 1988.

Guthrie, James W., ed. *School Finance and Practices in the 1980s: A Decade of Conflict*. Cambridge, Mass.: Ballinger, 1980.

Guthrie, James W., and Rodney J. Reed, *Educational Administration and Policy: Effective Leadership for American Education*. Englewood Cliffs, N.J.: Prentice-Hall, 1986.

Hentges, Joseph T. "The Politics of Superintendent School Board Linkages: A Study of Power, Participation, and Control." Paper presented at the annual meeting of the American Association of School Administrators, Dallas, March 1985.

Hill, David. "Christian Soldier." *Teacher Magazine*, November/December 1992, 18–21.

Hodgkinson, Christopher. *Educational Leadership: The Moral Art*. Albany: State University of New York Press, 1991.

Hollingshead, August B. *Elmstown's Youth: The Impact of Social Classes on Adolescents*. New York: John Wiley & Sons, 1949.

Hosman, Carol M., et al. "Assessment of Community Dissatisfaction: A Longitudinal Study of Electoral Conflict on School Boards." Paper presented at the annual meeting of the American Educational Research Association, Washington, D.C., April 1987.

Huberman, A. Michael, and Matthew D. Miles. *Innovation Up Close: How School Improvement Works*. New York: Plenum Press, 1984.

Hunter, Floyd. *Community Power Structure: A Study of Decision Makers*. Chapel Hill: University of North Carolina Press, 1953.

Hunter, Madeline. "Knowing, Teaching, and Supervision." In *Using What We Know About Teaching*, edited by P. L. Hosford, 169–92. Alexandria, Va.: Association for Supervision and Curriculum Development, 1984.

Iannacone, Laurence. *Politics in Education*. New York: Center for Applied Research in Education, Inc., 1967.

Iannacone, Laurence, and Frank Lutz. *Politics, Power and Policy*. Columbus, Ohio: Charles E. Merrill Publishing Co., 1970.

Immegart, Glenn L., and William L. Boyd, eds. *Problem Finding in Educational Administration*. Lexington, Mass.: Heath, 1979.

Inglis, William. *George F. Johnson and His Industrial Democracy*. 2d ed. New York: Huntington Press, 1948.

Institute for Educational Leadership. *School Boards: Strengthening Grass Roots Leadership*. Washington, D.C.: IEL Publications, 1986.

Johnson, George F. *E.J. Workers' Review*. 20 March 1919.

Johnson City: A Historical Review 1892–1976. In Your Home Library Historical collection, Johnson City, N.Y., 1976.

Johnson City Central School District Minutes. 13 March 1968.

Johnson City Central School District Minutes. 10 March 1970.

Johnson City Central School District Minutes. 20 December 1970.

Johnson City Central School District Minutes. 26 January 1971.

Johnson City Central School District Minutes. 23 February 1971.

Johnson City Central School District Minutes. 25 May 1971.

Johnson City Central School District Minutes. 10 May 1972.

Johnson City Central School District Minutes. 23 May 1972.

Johnson City Central School District Minutes. 23 October 1973.

Johnson City Central School District Minutes. 22 January 1974.

Johnson City Central School District Minutes. 16 November 1976.

Johnson City Central School District Minutes. 14 November 1978.

Johnson City Central School District Minutes. 14 December 1982.

Kandel, I. L., ed. *Educational Yearbook of the International Yearbook of the Institute of Teachers College, Columbia University.* New York: Macmillan, 1926.

Katz, Michael. *Class, Bureaucracy, and Schools: The Illusion of Educational Change in America.* New York: Praeger, 1971.

Kerr, Norman D. "The School Board as an Agency of Legitimation." *Sociology of Education* 38 (Fall 1954): 34–59.

Kimbrough, Ralph B. *Political Power and Educational Decision Making.* Chicago: Rand McNally, 1964.

Kirkendall, Richard S. "Discriminating Social, Economic, and Political Characteristics of Changing Versus Stable Policy-Making Systems in School Districts." Ph.D. diss., Claremont Graduate School, 1966.

Kirst, Michael W. "Effective Schools: Political Environment and Educational Policy." *Planning and Changing* 14 (Winter 1983): 234–44.

Kirst, Michael W., ed. *The Politics of Education at the Local, State, and Federal Levels.* Berkeley, Calif.: McCutchan, 1970.

Kojève, Alexandre. *Introduction to the Reading of Hegel.* New York: Basic Books, 1969.

Kreisberg, Seth. *Transforming Power: Domination, Empowerment, and Education.* Albany: State University of New York Press, 1992.

Kulik, J.A., C. C. Kulik, and P. A. Cohen. "A Meta-Analysis of Outcome Studies of Keller's Personalized System of Instruction." *American Psychologist* 34 **(date?)**: 307–18.

Lasswell, Harold D. *Politics: Who Gets What, When and How?* New York: McGraw-Hill, 1936

Levine, Daniel, and Robert Havighurst. *Society and Education.* 6th ed. Boston: Allyn and Bacon, 1980.

Lightfoot, Sara Lawrence. *The Good High School.* New York: Basic Books, 1983.

Luckett, R., et al. "How Men and Women Board Members Match Up." *American School Board Journal* 26 (January 1987).

Lukacs, John. *Historical Consciousness or The Remembered Past.* New York: Schocken Books, 1985.

Luksik, Peg, and Pamela Hobbs Hoffecker. *Outcome-Based Education: The State's Assault on Our Children's Values.* Lafayette, La.: Huntington House, 1995.

Lutz, Frank, and B. Hunt. "Predicting School Board Incumbent Defeat." Paper presented at the annual meeting of the American Educational Research Association, Los Angeles, Calif., April, 1982.

Lutz, Frank, and Joseph J. Azzarelli. *Struggle for Power in Education.* New York: The Center for Applied Research in Education, 1966.

Lutz, Frank, and Laurence Iannacone. "The Dissatisfaction Theory of American Democracy: A Guide for Politics in Local School Districts." Paper presented at the annual meeting of the American Association of School Administrators, San Francisco, Calif., February 1986.

——— *Public Participation in Local Schools.* Lexington, Mass.: Heath, 1978.

Lutz, Frank, and Lee-Yen Wang. "Predicting Public Dissatisfaction: A Study of School Board Member Defeat." *Educational Adminstrative Quarterly* 23, no. 1 (February 1987): 65–77.

Mamary, Albert. "The Outcomes-Driven Developmental Model." Document distributed at ODDM conference, Binghamton, N.Y., 1987.

Mann, Dale. *The Politics of Administrative Representation.* Lexington, Mass: Heath & Co., 1976.

Marshall, James D. "Foucault and Education." *Australian Journal of Education* 33, no.2 (August 1989): 99–113.

McCarty, Donald J., and Charles E. Ramsey. *The School Managers.* Westport, Conn.: Greenwood, 1971.

McClelland, David C. *Power: The Inner Experience.* New York: Irvington, 1975.

McGivney, Joseph H., and William Moynihan. "School and Community." *Teachers College Record* 74, no. 2 (December 1972): 209–24.

McLaren, Peter. *Life in Schools.* New York: Longman, 1989.

McPherson, Bruce R. et al. *Managing Uncertainty: Administrative Theory and Practice in Education.* Columbus, Ohio: Charles E. Merrill Pub. Co., 1986.

McPherson, Gertrude H. *Small Town Teacher.* Cambridge: Harvard University Press, 1972.

McQuaide, Judith, and Ann-Maureen Pliska. "The Challenge to Pennsylvania's Education Reform." *Educational Leadership* 51, no. 4 (December 1993/January 1994): 16–21.

Merelman, R.M. "Public Education and Social Structure: Three Modes of Adjustment." *Journal of Politics* 35 (1973): 798–829.

Miles, Matthew B., and Michael A. Huberman, *Qualitative Data Analysis: A Sourcebook of New Methods.* Beverly Hills, Calif.: Sage Publications, 1984.

Miller, Jean Baker. *Toward a New Psychology of Women.* Boston: Beacon Press, 1976.

Miller, Terry M., ed. *Working Lives: Broome County, New York, 1800–1930.* Binghamton, N.Y.: Roberson Center for the Arts and Sciences, 1980.

Minar, David W. "The Community Basis of Conflict in School System Politics." *American Sociological Review* 31 (December 1966): 822–34.

Mitchell, Brad. "Children, Youth, and Restructured Schools: Views from the Field." In part 2 of *Educational Leadership and Changing Contexts of Families, Communities, and Schools,* edited by Brad Mitchell and Luvern L. Cunningham. Eighty-ninth Yearbook of the National Society for the Study of Education. Chicago: University of Chicago Press, 1990.

Mitchell, Douglas E. "Ideological Structure and School Policy-making." Ph.D. diss., Claremont Graduate School, 1972.

Mitchell, Stephen M., and Samuel B. Bacharach, "The Politics of School Board Turnover: An Exploratory Study." Ithaca, N.Y: Cornell University (ERIC Document Reproduction Service No. 243 177), 1983.

Moen, Allen W. "Superintendent Turnover as Predicted by School Board Incumbent Defeat in Pennsylvania's Partisan Elections." Ph.D. diss., Pennsylvania State University, 1971.

Mullins, Carolyn. "School District Consolidation: Odds are 2 to 1, It'll Get You." *American School Board Journal* 160, no. 11 (November 1973): 23–26, 57.

Muth, Rodney. "Toward an Integrative Theory of Educational Power and Education Organizations." *Educational Administration Quarterly* 20 (Spring 1984): 25–42.

Muth, Rodney, and Azumi, Jann. "School Reform: Whither Boards of Education?" Paper presented at the annual meeting of the American Educational Research Association, Washington, D.C., April 1987.

National Commission on Excellence in Education. *A Nation at Risk.* Washington, D.C.: U.S. Government Printing Office, 1966.

National School Board Association. "School Boards Not Passive." *School Board News,* November 1986, 1, 3.

Newman, Fred, and Lois Holzman. *Lev Vygotsky: Revolutionary Scientist.* New York: Routledge, 1993.

Olson, Lynn. "Local School Boards Lose Power, Prestige, New Study Asserts." *Education Week* 6, no. 10 (November 1986): 1, 16.

Owen, Robert. *The Life of Robert Owen Written by Himself, with Selections from His Writing and Correspondence.* Vol. 1. New York: A. M. Kelley, 1967. Originally published in 1857.

Noddings, Nel. "An Ethic of Caring and Its Implications for Instructional Arrangements." In *The Educational Feminism Reader,* edited by Lynda Stone. New York: Routledge, 1994.

Partners All: A Pictorial Narrative of an Industrial Democracy. Photographed by R. Clikins. New York: Huntington Corp., 1938.

Passow, Harry A. "Secondary Education Reform: Retrospect and Prospect." Paper presented at the Julius and Rosa Sachs Memorial Lectures, Teachers College, Columbia University, 7–8 April 1976.

Pearson, Jim B., and Edgar Fuller, eds. *Education in the States: Nationwide Development Since 1900.* Washington, D.C.: NEA, 1969.

Peshkin, Alan. *Growing Up American: Schooling and the Survival of Community.* Chicago: The University of Chicago Press, 1978.

Peterson, Paul E. *The Politics of School Reform, 1870–1940.* Chicago: University of Chicago Press, 1985.

———. *Review of Research in Education.* Edited by F. N. Kerlinger and J. B. Carroll. Itasca, Ill.: F. E. Peacock, 1974.

Pitkin, Hannah F. *The Concept of Representation.* Berkeley: University of California Press, 1967.

Pliska, Ann-Maureen, and Judith McQuaide. "Pennsylviania's Battle for Student Learning Outcomes." *Educational Leadership* 51, no. 6 (March 1994): 66–69.

Presseisen, Barbara Z., and Alex Kozulin. "Mediated Learning—The Contributions of Vygotsky and Feuerstein in Theory and Practice." Paper presented at the annual meeting of the American Educational Research Association, San Francisco, April 1992.

Rada, Roger D., and Richard O. Carlson. "Community Dissatisfaction and School Governance." Paper presented at the annual meeting of the American Educational Research Association, Chicago, Ill., April 1985.

Rallis, Sharon. "Professional Teachers and Restructured Schools: Leadership Challenges." In pt. 2 of *Educational Leadership and Changing Context of Families, Communities, and Schools*, edited by Brad Mitchell and Luvern L. Cunningham. Eighty-ninth Yearbook of the National Society for the Study of Education. Chicago: University of Chicago Press, 1990.

Ravitch, Diane. *The Troubled Crusade: American Education, 1945–1980*. New York: Basic Books, 1983.

Reid, William A. *Thinking About the Curriculum*. London: Routledge & Kegan Paul, 1978.

Rodgers, William. *Think: A Biography of the Watsons and IBM*. New York: Stein and Day, 1969.

Rosenblum, Sheila, and Karen S Louis. *Stability and Change: Innovation in an Educational Context*. Cambridge, Mass.: ABT Associates, 1981.

Rosenthal, Alan. "Pedagogues and Power." In *Governing Education: A Reader on Politics, Power and School Policy*. Edited by A. Rosenthal, 291–313. Garden City, N.Y.: Anchor Books, 1969.

Rowe, Lawrence, and Frank V. Alessi. "The Outcomes-Driven Developmental Model." Johnson City, N.Y.: Johnson City Central School District, 1993.

Sarason, Seymour. *The Predictable Failure of Educational Reform*. San Francisco: Jossey-Bass, 1991.

———. *Schooling in America: Scapegoat and Salvation*. New York: The Free Press, 1983.

Saul, Richard S. "An American Entreprenuer." Excerpt of dissertation published in the *Sun-Bulletin*, 5 December 1966 through 23 December 1966, in the Your Home Library collection.

———. "An American Entrepreneur." Ph.D. diss., Syracuse University, 1967.

Schlechty, Phillip C. *Reaching for Excellence: An Effective Schools Sourcebook*. Edited by Regina M. J. Kyle. Washington, D.C.: U.S. Government Printing Office, May 1985.

Schmoker, Michael J., and Richard B. Wilson, *Total Quality Education*. Bloomington, Ind.: Phi Delta Kappa Educational Foundation, 1993.

Schon, Donald A. *The Reflective Turn: Case Studies In and On Educational Practice*. New York: Teachers College Press, 1991.

Sergiovanni, Thomas J., and Fred D. Carver. *The New School Executive*. New York: Harper and Row, 1980.

Sergiovanni, Thomas J., et al. *Educational Governance and Administration.* Englewood Cliffs, N.J.: Prentice-Hall, 1980.

Sergiovanni, Thomas J., and John E. Corbally, eds. *Leadership and Organizational Culture: New Perspectives on Administrative Theory and Practice.* Urbana: University of Illinois Press, 1984.

Seward, William F., ed. *Binghamton and Broome County, New York: A History.* Vol. 3. New York: Lewis Historical Pub. Co., 1924.

Silver, Paula F. *Educational Administration: Theoretical Perspectives on Practice and Research.* New York: Harper & Row, 1983.

Simonds, Robert L. "A Plea for the Children." *Educational Leadership* 51, no. 4 (December 1993/January 1994): 12–15.

Sizer, Theodore R. *Horace's Compromise: The Dilemma of the American High School.* Boston: Houghton Mifflin, 1984.

Smith, Gerald R. *The Valley of Opportunity: A Pictorial History of the Greater Binghamton Area.* Norfolk, Va.: The Donning Co., 1988.

Smith, Nancy J. "Reconsiderations of Dynamic Administration: The Collected Papers of Mary Parker Follett." *Educational Studies* 25, no. 3 (Fall 1994): 199-209.

"Some Significant Dates in the History of Broome County, New York." Binghamton, N.Y.: Broome County Chamber of Commerce, 1984.

Spady, William G. "Choosing Outcomes of Significance." *Educational Leadership* 51, no. 6 (March 1994): 18–22.

———. "Outcome-Based Instructional Management: A Sociological Perspective." Paper prepared for the National Institute of Education, January 1981.

Spady, William, James H. Block, Helen E. Efthim, and Robert B. Burns. *Building Effective Mastery Schools.* New York: Longman, 1989.

Spring, Joel. *American Education.* New York: Longman, 1989.

Starhawk. *Dreaming the Dark: Magic, Sex, and Politics.* Boston: Beacon Press, 1988.

Stevenson, Harold W., and James W. Stigler. *The Learning Gap: Why Our Schools Are Failing and What We Can Learn from Japanese and Chinese Education.* New York: Summit Books, 1992.

Suarez, Maritza M. de. "An Ex Post Facto Study of Achievement Pattern Under Mastery Learning." Ph.D. diss., Syracuse University, 1985.

Tanner, Daniel, and Laurel N. Tanner. *Curriculum Development: Theory into Practice.* New York: Macmillan, 1975.

Tarbell, Ida M. "'Humans 90% Good' Says George F." *Red Cross Magazine,* January 1920.

Thompson, John T. *Policymaking in American Public Education: A Framework for Analysis.* Englewood Cliffs, N.J.: Prentice-Hall, 1976.

Tocqueville, Alexis de. *Democracy in America.* Translated by George Lawrence. Edited by J. P. Mayer and Max Lerner. New York: Harper and Row, 1966.

Toennies, Ferdinand. *Community and Society*. Translated from the German by C. P. Loomis. New York: Harper and Row, 1967. Originally published as *Gemeinschaft und Gesellschaft*.

Tucker, Harvey J., and L. Harmon Zeigler. *Professionals versus the Public: Attitudes, Communication and Response in School Districts*. New York: Longman, 1980.

Tyack, David B. *The One Best System: A History of American Urban Education*. Cambridge: Harvard University Press, 1974.

Tyack, David B., and Elisabeth Hansot. *Managers of Virtue: Public School Leadership in American, 1820–1980*. New York: Basic Books, 1982.

United States. Bureau of the Census. *1960 Census of Population and Housing*. Census Tracts for Binghamton, N.Y. Washington, D.C.: U.S. Government Printing Office, 1961.

———. Bureau of the Census. *1970 Census of Population and Housing*. Census Tracts for Binghamton, N.Y.–PA. SMSA. Washington, D.C.: U.S. Government Printing Office, 1971.

———. Bureau of the Census. *1980 Census of Population and Housing*. Census Tracts for Binghamton, N.Y.–PA. SMSA. Washington, D.C., 1981.

———. Bureau of the Census. *Social and Economic Characteristics of Metropolitan and Nonmetropolitan Populations: 1977 and 1970*. Washington, D.C.: U.S. Government Printing Office, 1978.

———. Department of Commerce. *Statistical Abstract of the United States*. Washington, D.C.: U.S. Government Printing Office, 1993.

Valley of Fair Play. Johnson City, N.Y.: Johnson City Publishing Co., 1919.

van Geel, Tyll. *Authority to Control the School Program*. Lexington, Mass: Heath, 1976.

———. "Parental Preferences and the Politics of Spending Educational Funds." *Teachers College Record* 79 (1979).

Vickery, Tom Rusk. "Evaluating a Mastery Learning High School." *Persoon En Gemeenschap* 40, no. 10 (1987/88): 803.

———. "Excellence in an Outcomes-Driven School District." Effective Schools Program Validation, Grant 407–84–02–025–038, September 1985.

———. "Learning From an Outcomes-Driven School District." *Educational Leadership* 45 (February 1988): 52–56.

———. "ODDM: A Workable Model of Total School Improvement." *Educational Leadership* 47 (April 1990): 67–70.

Vidich, Arthur J., and Joseph Bensman. *Small Town in Mass Society*. 2d ed. Princeton: Princeton University Press, 1968. Originally published in 1958.

"Village of Johnson City Comprehensive Development Plan." Binghamton, N.Y.: Broome County Planning Office, 1967.

Vygotsky, L. S. *Mind in Society: The Development of Higher Psychological Processes*. Edited by Michael Cole, Vera John-Steiner, and Ellen Souberman. Cambridge: Harvard University Press, 1978.

Walden, John C. "School Board Changes and Involuntary Superintendent Turnover." Ph.D. diss., Claremont Graduate School, 1966.

Warner, W. Lloyd, et al. *Democracy in Jonesville*. New York: Harper and Row, 1949.

Warren, Roland L. *The Community in America*. Chicago: Rand McNally, 1963.

Warren, Roland L., et al. *The Structure of Urban Reform*. Lexington, Mass.: Heath & Co., 1974.

Weick, Karl E. "Educational Organizations as Loosely Coupled Systems." *Administrative Science Quarterly* 21 (1976): 1–19.

Weil, Simone. *The Need for Roots*. Boston: Beacon Press, 1952.

Wertsch, James V. *Voices of the Mind: A Sociocultural Approach to Mediated Action*. Cambridge: Harvard University Press, 1991.

Wirt, Frederick M. "What Do State Laws Say About Local Control?" *Phi Delta Kappan*, April 1978, 517–20.

Wirt, Frederick, and Michael W. Kirst, *The Political Web of American Schools*. Boston: Little, Brown, 1972.

———. *Schools in Conflict*. Berkeley, Calif.: McCutchan Pub. Co., 1982.

Wissler, Dorothy Fast. "Decentralization of Decision-Making in Riverside Unified School District: An Historical Analysis." Ph.D. diss., University of California at Riverside, June 1984.

Zahavi, Gerald. "Workers, Managers, and Welfare Capitalism: The Shoeworkers and Tanners of Endicott Johnson, 1880–1950." Ph.D. diss., Syracuse University, December 1983.

Zeigler, L. Harmon. "School Board Research: The Problems and the Prospects." Paper presented at the annual meeting of the National School Boards Association, Miami Beach, Fla., April 1975.

Zeigler, L. Harmon, and M. Kent. Jennings. *Governing American Schools*. North Scituate, Mass.: Duxbury Press, 1974.

Zeigler, L. Harmon, Ellen Kehoe, and Jane Reisman. *City Managers and School Superintendents: Response to Community Conflict*. New York: Praeger Special Studies, 1985.

Zirkel, Perry A., and Scott C. Greenwood, "Effective Schools and Effective Principals: Effective Research?" *Teachers College Record* 89, no. 2 (Winter 1987): 255–67.

Acknowledgments

To be a soul remembering good friends is a happy conclusion to one's work. In the completion of this research and book, I have been fortunate to have had the assistance of friends, colleagues, acquaintances, and family.

Without the help of the students and staff of the Johnson City Central School District and the citizens of Johnson City, this book would not exist. To them, I extend my appreciation for the information and time they granted me and their work in recreating their schools and community. I especially want to thank Dr. Albert Mamary for granting me access to district materials and for his intellectual curiosity and kind spirit. I am also deeply indebted to the district secretaries—Jo Wells, Arlene Karaim, and Wilma Klysch—for their openness and assistance during my many trips to Johnson City. Anne and Jack Shelton, residents of Johnson City, shared their home with me during several of these visits and provided introductions to the many community members I interviewed. I sincerely thank the both of them for their hospitality and generosity.

Tom Rusk Vickery introduced me to the Johnson City Schools and was an excellent advisor through the arduous dissertation process. John Briggs and Gerald Grant's comments and insights gave me significant direction, encouragement, and advice during my research on this project. I reserve special praise and profound gratitude to both Eugene Provenzo and Lois Patton for their belief in the value of this work and for their encouragement and guidance through the many stages of the book. I appreciate the support of Millersville University and its granting me released time for this project. I also wish to acknowledge the help of Dr. John R. Champlin, Dr. Albert Mamary, Partners for Quality Learning, the National Center for Outcome Based Education, and the Johnson City Central Schools in the publication of this book.

Each revision of this manuscript improved greatly with Elizabeth Gonzalez's editing. Her love of language and her skill in its use smoothed many an awkward phrase of mine. I am deeply grateful to my husband, Dan, and children, Anne and Des, for their patience and understanding as this project grew through the years. Their love and support have sustained me.

Index